PENGUIN BOOKS

A LIFE OF ONE'S OWN

ILANA SIMONS received her PhD in literature in 2003 and teaches at The New School in New York City. She won the Willy Gorrissen Award for Teaching Excellence and the Molberger Fellowship for modernist scholarship while a graduate student at New York University. She moderates the online Barnes & Noble Book Clubs, and is also currently in training as a clinical psychologist.

a life of one's own

A GUIDE TO ORIGINAL LIVING THROUGH THE
WORK AND WISDOM OF VIRGINIA WOOLF

Ilana Simons

PENGUIN BOOKS

PENGUIN BOOKS
Published by the Penguin Group
Penguin Group (USA) Inc., 375 Hudson Street, New York, New York 10014, U.S.A.,
Penguin Group (Canada), 90 Eglinton Avenue East, Suite 700, Toronto, Ontari, Canada
M4P 2Y3, (a division of Pearson Penguin Canada Inc.); Penguin Books Ltd, 80 Strand,
London WC2R 0RL, England; Penguin Ireland, 25 St Stephen's Green, Dublin 2, Ireland
(a division of Penguin Books Ltd); Penguin Group (Australia), 250 Camberwell Road,
Camberwell, Victoria 3124, Australia (a division of Pearson Australia Group Pty. Ltd);
Penguin Books India Pvt Ltd, 11 Community Centre, Panchsheel Park, New Delhi – 110 017,
India; Penguin Group (NZ), 67 Apollo Drive, Rosedale, North Shore 0745, Auckland,
New Zealand (a division of Pearson New Zealand Ltd.);Penguin Books (South Africa)
(Pty) Ltd, 24 Sturdee Avenue, Rosebank, Johannesburg 2196, South Africa

Penguin Books Ltd, Registered Offices:
80 Strand, London WC2R 0RL, England

First Published in Penguin Books 2007

10   9   8   7   6   5   4   3   2   1

LIBRARY OF CONGRESS CATALOGING IN PUBLICATION DATA
Simons, Ilana R.
A life of one's own : a guide to better living through the work and wisdom of Virginia
Woolf / Ilana R. Simons.
p. cm.
Includes bibliographical references.
ISBN 978-0-14-311225-9
1. Woolf, Virginia, 1882–1941—Appreciation.   2. Wisdom in literature.   3. Life skills.
I Title.
PR6045.O72Z87645 2007
823'.912—dc22 2006052724

Printed in the United States of America
Set in Spectrum Mt   •   Designed by Sabrina Bowers

FOR VICKI AND BOB, parents who encouraged me to a life of my own. When I was nine and they renovated the house, they said, "You're going to get a room of your own. You don't yet know why you'll love this. But you will."

Acknowledgments

Thank you to agent Neeti Madan and editor David Cashion, who liked what I sent and stuck with me until it was understandable to others, too. Thank you to Robin Mookerjee, for entrusting me with the job I love; to John Maynard for guiding my dissertation; to Fred Ulfers for giving me a way to read modernist books; and to Vicki Simons, for giving me the writing feedback that's changed me most. I love the people who've made me feel alive at all the crucial crossroads: Kate Walat, Rob Marinelli, Josh Mason, Bob Holman, Valmonte Simone Weiss Sprout, Patrick Mangina Bucklew, Peg Alford, Brian Slater, Jim Rotondi,

Richard Ryan, Jonathan Liebson, Allen Jones, David Orlowski, Marge, Eric, Josh, and Youn Hadar, and Leigh, Todd C., Jane, and Onofre Torres. I'm thankful to my students at New York University and The New School, who are daring and generous with their own ideas, and to the psychology faculty at The New School. Most of all, thank you to Vicki, Bob, and Matt for being the center of my world, and to Larry, the wisest person in New York, who comforts and teaches me on a daily basis.

Contents

Acknowledgments   *vii*

Introduction   *xi*

CHAPTER 1: *Speak Up*   *1*

CHAPTER 2: *Accept Solitude*   *15*

CHAPTER 3: *Shut Down*   *37*

CHAPTER 4: *Take on Challenging Friendships*   *51*

CHAPTER 5: *Find Steady Support*   *65*

CHAPTER 6: *Work Hard, Even Without a Sign of Success*   *75*

CHAPTER 7: *Lie to Encourage Your Friends*   *89*

CHAPTER 8: *Find a Political Voice*   *101*

CHAPTER 9: *Be Aware of Prejudice*   *113*

CHAPTER 10: *Change Routines*   *123*

CHAPTER 11: *Read Your Partner*   *143*

CHAPTER 12: *Make Use of Time*   *153*

CHAPTER 13: *Read and Be More*   *163*

Epilogue   *185*

Notes   *193*

Introduction

Virginia Woolf is an icon with a shaky reputation. She's frequently portrayed as a troubled woman who loved the obscure and abstract—some say too much. She earned her fame through writing novels that developed Modernism, a period that shifted literature away from the Victorian Realist's description of the physical world to a description of what life *feels* like as it happens. She described the mind's ride through its smallest bends and mood shifts.

Woolf was also a journalist and a printer of other people's books, a diarist, a letter-writer, and a partygoer. She was a member of the Bloomsbury set, a group of twentieth-century London intellectuals including Lytton Strachey, Duncan Grant, and John Maynard Keynes that was known for a progressive mind-set, but was also criticized for an elitist aesthetic. And Woolf is certainly known for her depression, having killed herself at fifty-nine through drowning in the River Ouse outside her summer home.

However, despite the darker elements of her life, Virginia Woolf has been invaluable for countless writers, artists, and readers over the years. I, personally, came to appreciate her art as a literature professor, teaching her novels alongside the other big books of the Modernist era. Increasingly aware that great literature is frequently a study of the human head, I followed that line professionally, too, and am in training as a clinical psychologist. Woolf sits at the intersection of these interests: helping us know ourselves through books. In fact, in neither psychology nor literature do I know a writer who does a better job of describing the movements of the mind and emotions than she does. She has the observational genius and communicative skills to help us look at our lives with a fresh, sharp focus.

It's not frequently enough, though, that we credit Woolf's focus on the personal with the political importance she thought it to have. Although she was sometimes accused of having a bourgeois aesthetic, Woolf saw her study of how we relate to one another as a profoundly political gesture. She resented the dogma or rigid external parading of politics as it existed in her time; in turn, she wrote to revalue equally crucial social activities: hearing what goes unspoken, tending to our partners, offering support. She fought for some typically political ends, too—arguing against Hitler and war; asking for better salaries and education for women in her historically important nonfiction book *A Room of One's Own*. But the great morality behind Woolfian style is her shift from political dogma to the personal: to see psychology at the root of all we do; to describe even governments as outgrowths of personalities; to give new credit to interpersonal skills, which we often undervalue.

· · · · ·

WOOLF'S NEED TO PUT the *mind* on the page was a mission partly shaped by her biology. No fan would try to show that Woolf was wise about life with evidence that she was always happy. She suffered from what we'd diagnose today as bipolar disorder, routinely moving between bouts of serious depression, in which she'd hallucinate, suffer headaches, and lose her appetite; and mania, in which she wrote with a fabulous fury. Although she did admit her condition to be a sickness, she also knew it gave her a take on personality that meant prime positioning for her work. Woolf's focus was to show that we all undergo, but underplay, some version of the emotional ride she lived so clearly. Our emotional needs affect everything we do—how we love, philosophize, govern nations—more than we often admit. She worked to help us own this condition: to know ourselves by diving in, with frenetic force, to see the inside. Her suicide is a sign of the amount she dared to feel, but it does not diminish the vision she left—her wisdom about conversation, ambition, and mutual respect.

People sometimes feel put-off by Woolf because they cannot see beyond the icon and are frightened by what they perceive as her unfathomable depths and untouchable genius. That image is certainly a grander one than she would have felt comfortable with. In reality, she was self-taught. She might have grown up in an intellectual family, with a well-known biographer for a father and a mother from a successful publishing family, but other than a few tutors, she didn't go to school. Her brothers attended Cambridge, and partly because she was a woman, she stayed at home and read the family's books in her third-floor London bedroom. She loved the solitude, but had a sometimes-paralyzing respect for the Literary Greats her father valued. She wrote to help readers encounter books through emotion, to overcome the fear of vaulted intellect or academic precedent. She managed to create books that map the corners of our minds—so helped us know each other more than we would without good books.

· · · · ·

WHEN ALL IS SAID and done, if Woolf had one ethic about living, it was probably the reminder she scribbled to herself in her diary on March 8, 1941, just three weeks before her death: "Observe perpetually. Observe the oncoming of age. Observe greed. Observe my own despondency." Watch openly, Woolf says, not just by judging others, but especially by including yourself in the mix, watching yourself watching. For her, this was a moral imperative and a stance that makes her fiction practically relevant. She wanted to see what was raw, even ugly, about ourselves. She would watch herself engage in conversations, and stomach her own show of ego or hypocrisy. If it was human, she wanted to put it on the page. What emerged was a series of books that show us our beauties and shortcomings, an undoctored map to how we move in everything from family spats to politics. If Woolf is anything to me, she's a psychologist without the technical lingo, an artist who can also be called a life guide.

Over the course of a vigilant life, Woolf left volumes

packed with the world's most useful art and detritus: books, essays, diaries, and letters offering valuable descriptions of how we live, think, and know each other. *A Life of One's Own* is essentially a tribute to her voice gleaned from all those pages, a sketch of the places I and others have heard and used Woolf's advice—from inside family talks and friendship negotiations, to political decisions and career moves. Ultimately, I have tried to gather up the insights from this life of work to explain the wisdom that's hit me hardest and can change us most.

a life of one's own

CHAPTER 1

Speak Up

START WITH A STORY from Virginia's own life, as she recorded it in a memoir. We'll find her at sixteen, already self-scrutinizing and smart from it. "Ginia" (the nickname her father liked) and her brothers and sisters—three full and four half siblings—grew up in a dark, five-story London house. The boys left during the day to go to college or work; her sister Vanessa left to paint with a tutor; her mother worked with the poor; her father wrote books; and Virginia decided, early on, to be a writer. She didn't go to college but spent most of her days in her room, studying books that she borrowed from her father's saturated study. The house grew silent after breakfast, and needing to entertain herself, she read. She also needed to cope with a lot of loss in the early years. Her mother, sister, and father all passed away by the time she was twenty-two.

She was close to her full siblings, but always felt a radical difference from the sons from her mother's previous marriage—Gerald and George. These half brothers were socialites, party-lovers more than readers, and they made a grand show of it. They used to tug the two sisters, Virginia and Vanessa, into their action. After a day of work, they'd try to drag them to parties in the evenings.

At sixteen, Virginia was too cheap to buy new dresses and also self-conscious about being cheap, so she hated going out at night with her brothers. She assumed no one at the grand Victorian salons would empathize with her intellectual passion, her love of books. But George would call her down from her bedroom in the late afternoon, tell her about his last late night out, and occasionally drive her to a party somewhere in London. Her experience at parties became a central focus in her writing, and to see why, catch her in descriptions from her own memoir "22 Hyde Park Gate":

Sitting at the Countess of Carnarvon's dinner on Bruton Street, London, at about 1898 are Virginia and George, flanked by older decorated women. The hostess is dressed in black because she's mourning her husband. Once vice-reine of Canada, and of Ireland, having inherited diamonds from Marie Antoinette, she's only lightly decorated now, with a small necklace. A Lady Popham of Littlecote is on the other side, also in a sort of mourning because her husband, a descendant of Henry the Eighth, is in an insane asylum. The women chat as they nibble their rolls.

Virginia's already prepped to feel like an "outsider," which is a word she would later focus on in her writing. At the party, she was basically hyperconscious of the division between her own head (as an intellectual teen, fearing no soul at this table could love her love, books) and the superficial society talk that shot from one yapping mouth to another. She felt disappointed in a solitary way—as if she had a more complex and active mind than people around her did.

At sixteen, she probably just felt disenchantment with stiff older people, but Woolf would later write novels to describe what was happening. Trying to feel confident, looking around the table, she saw a divide between *me* and *them*. She exaggerated the difference between herself and others, putting a gulf between the party talk out-there and her own thinking. She could, after all, backstroke through her own silence and privacy: the reasons she was worthwhile, the words she chose *not* to speak, her memories, and her sense of being a person.

No one has access to other heads, so your own mind *feels* like the most active one in the room. This is a line of discourse in philosophy that's run from at least Descartes, who described the delusions of privacy in the seventeenth century, to its peak in the twentieth-century phenomenologists like Sartre, who focused on the experience of time's passing. These philosophers defined a basic source of alienation: the difference between feeling life happen within, and watching it happen, across the dinner table or across the room. Our minds come with their feelings; and other people seem simpler—less complex. You can imagine you're the wisest person in the room, and others are just banging from thing to thing.

· · · · ·

WOOLF WROTE FICTION THAT explores this difference. She took it further, too, saying we feel a bigger sense of our own perfection when we watch other people but judge them quietly, without speaking, ourselves. For example, see me at the Thanksgiving table at seventeen, while my older cousin stands and gives a toast. Since I'm just home from freshman year of college, I'm serious—

I have decided to *fight hypocrisy*. When cousin Tim slaps his hands together, belly laughs, and brags about his three-day hike up the Pyrenees, I think I see through him. With a new baby boy, Tim's become the Man of the family who makes the toasts. He's *proud*, I think, *toasting not just to say "I like you all" but "I'm impressive."* When he sneaks a glimpse of his profile in the mirror, I tell myself I won't be as vain as he is. I protect my freshman sense of self by defining us as opposites: I'm conscious of how I am in the world; he's unaware of how he gobbles up the spotlight.

Woolf would say I protect myself by silently distancing others. My privacy feels unique. But Woolf will go on to explain that I'm more like my cousin than I think. I'm only "perfect" when I'm quiet, and if I actually got up to give a toast, I'd see my similarities to cousin Tim. I'd see how I also gloat with the spotlight, how I also sneak a look at myself in the mirror when I can. I might feel proud in ways I don't name yet. But I'd need to engage in real conversation to see how living *happens* outside of my comforting silence.

· · · · ·

WOOLF'S POINT IS THAT we know ourselves through interacting as much as just through thinking. We tend to judge others when we're silent; we learn more about ourselves and the world when we relax our defenses and *talk*. This idea has excited many of history's big minds. The famously complex philosopher Hegel, for instance, also said that when we hold back with others, we're often just being defensive. When I'm silent at a dinner party or a business meeting, Hegel meant, I reserve my right to idealize about my talents. It's only when we actually speak and act that we come to see what's real, not just imagined, about us. In his writing, Hegel developed a character called the Beautiful Soul, and this Beautiful Soul, like Woolf and me in our teens, protects his self-image by staying quiet at places like the dinner table. The Beautiful Soul doesn't want to enter too many conversations, because he thinks he's deliciously *different* from people around him. He doesn't want to use the words everyone uses, like "lonely," as in "I feel lonely" or "happy," as in "I'm happy." He thinks those descriptions might suit other lives, but they couldn't convey the inner feeling of *his world*. His view feels richer than a stranger's is.

For a while, the Beautiful Soul protects himself by resisting conversations that would reveal him. But friends finally force him to enter their world and say what he thinks. He has to jump into the dirty public pool of dictionary words, the terms we all use to describe what goes on in private. The process breaks him down, Hegel writes, but it also gives a new perspective on who he is.

Being open with others shows how once-private ideas actually play out in the world. Someone interprets your sentence in a way you didn't mean—showing that what you say has many connotations. Someone else—who you always considered humorless—actually makes you laugh. Conversation teaches us something when it upsets expectations.

Woolf showed how conversation teaches us in her novel *To the Lighthouse.* In that book she places a self-important thirty-three-year-old, Lily, next to an equally arrogant young man, Tansley, at a dinner party. Lily and Tansley both keep to themselves, feeling as if everyone else at the table is categorically different—chattier and simpler. Lily looks at Tansley and thinks he's more arrogant than she is. Calling him impossibly *male*, she goes on to define men in general as more arrogant and needy than women. When she turns her back to Tansley to mark their difference, he in turn ignores her.

But the tenderness in Woolf's scene comes through the fact that these two young people are making life hard for themselves by claiming they're so original. The fact is, they both essentially want the same thing—a crumb of attention. They're still idealistic, holding out for a perfect form of recognition, but what they need is the casual chat that makes a dinner party work. Both Lily and Tansley want someone at the table to turn their way, eyes wide, and ask a question. "What do you do, Lily?" or "Tell me about yourself, Tansley." But that sort of noticing actually comes in an ordinary conversation—and the longer these intellectual idealists hold out for pristine recognition, the hungrier they'll get for contact.

· · · · ·

MOST TALK TEACHES AND fulfills us. At sixteen, Virginia was first suspicious of the party talk at Carnarvon's table. But soon she saw that her defensiveness was a waste. After protecting her privacy for a while, Virginia was nudged to talk. Spying the teenager's anxiety, the hostess did the favor of asking her a few encouraging things. "Do you like to paint?" she said. The woman to her left helped out: "Do you like to read?" Virginia was polite at first, but when she answered, the very action of opening her mouth helped. She felt one word tumble into a race of words; she even went on to spout a theory about lack of emotion in the modern world. Conversation, she went on to say in all of her books, would feed her more than she imagines.

· · · · ·

HEGEL AND WOOLF ARE both interested in what we get when we let down our defenses and just enter the game. They think egoists are deluded, naming opposites or enemies when they shouldn't. It's smart to disown statements like "He's my nemesis" and "He's impossibly dumb," because the accusations are distancing and limit interaction.

I learned about how barriers can actually starve me when I heard the idea from my mother, before reading it in Woolf. After that dinner where my cousin gave a toast, I went to the kitchen with my mother to do dishes and vented: "He's so proud of himself now. He wants attention, and it's so obvious. It pisses me off." I imagined she'd rally with me: women against the egotistical young men.

But she kept piling dishes into the machine. Finally she looked at me, furrowing her brows: "And. He likes attention. So what." (She echoed Mrs. Ramsay, who, staring at a moping dinner guest, thinks, "Why not. . . . Let [him].")

My mother was hopelessly *casual*, I thought; *she should respect herself more*. She should *fight* these guys who demanded attention without being able to say it, who parade their stuff while women support them.

Like me, my mother might have resented the unspoken gender dynamics, but she also saw the immaturity in my own fighting mode. She was at a different place than I was—able to see some greed in all of us. She saw my cousin play out a (well-meaning) gesture for attention, and she didn't have to define it or beat him up for it. With her "so what" she broke the divide—told me I was pulling the same dynamic; I was running to the kitchen to get her attention. I'd hoped she'd turn to me with respect: *You're so surprisingly intelligent in your analysis of men!*

Mom knew that at least my cousin had been realistic enough about how attention works to just stand at the table, around everyone, and talk, even though it exposed him. I was more suspicious about exposure. I'd come to the privacy of the kitchen to bargain for a purer spotlight.

She wanted me to let down my fists in marking differences, to be able to say *he's hungry for applause* but not turn it into a tight-laced argument about his inhumanity.

· · · · ·

KNOW WHAT THIS MEANS. It also means we can be easier with ourselves. ("For the hundred and fiftieth time Lily . . . had to renounce the experiment [of distancing herself] and be nice" to the dinner guest beside her in Woolf's novel.) My mother was essentially telling me to say my ideas if I had them. Tap your glass, stand, and speak, even if it bares the ugly truth about you, that you like attention. She was telling me to let myself look demanding or silly sometimes. It's better to expose what you've got than spend all your energy avoiding situations that make you vulnerable.

· · · · ·

THE STRONGEST MOMENT I ever had with a therapist of mine was when he said this: "You manage to be *open*." He connected shooting from the gut with health—an idea that relaxed me. It's relieving to talk openly without fear of what you still have to learn.

· · · · ·

WOOLF'S HEROINES IN HER novels are the hostesses who are big enough to like ordinary people, which means they even welcome friends with sloppy habits. Of course people's personality quirks sometimes bother these heroines, too, but Woolf's Mrs. Ramsay and Mrs. Dalloway, for instance, would rather have people show their true selves at their parties than freeze up just to avoid embarrassment. Mrs. Ramsay is a heroine because she fosters activity for even her twisted friends. She looks around her own dinner, at the friends she's invited, and sees a group of neurotics. On one side of her sit Lily and Tansley, ignoring each other because they claim to be opposites. Then there's old Augustus, so socially awkward that he orders a second soup when everyone else wants the next course. And there sits her husband, who's self-centered and annoyed by Augustus's faux pas. But Mrs. Ramsay's social talent is that (though she sometimes wants to kill these fools) she doesn't think she's utterly more developed than they are. She has a dinner because she knows *this is who we are*, and she loves the diversity of it.

In fact, Woolf considered the dinner party the one epic stage in her books—a more fundamental test of what's human than some vaulted battlefield or perfect courtroom or regal scene. The party cuts people down off their professional posts, asks how they look other people in the face, unprotected by education and occupation. The dinner brings us together around the basics, asking every member of the family to show her character and admit her needs.

In Woolf's landscape, you get human by admitting you're more than one self: You can feel precious inside but you're not only that private self when you speak. The ego I deny pokes out whenever my mouth is in motion. Oh well. Part of this message is demeaning: If you think you're smart or considerate, you're not categorically special. But most of it is encouraging: Your ideas don't need to be perfectly formed before you speak them. Woolf tells the thoughtful girl in the corner to enter in—not just to judge, but to turn to her cousin, even when she doesn't like his story, tap his elbow, and tell him something.

CHAPTER 2

Accept Solitude

WOOLF SAYS WE HAVE to speak up—by actually talking and interacting with friends, demonstrate what makes us like them. But there are also limits in this vision, a darker claim at the root of her work. Namely, you're alone. You reach out to people with a hope for solid connections, and sometimes get them. But as frequently, you misread and misjudge the people you know. You see a face across the table and connect with her through words, but a lot gets missed. It's a shame, but true, and Woolf says happiness only comes when we accept that we make limited, flashing connections with other people.

· · · · ·

DROP YOURSELF INTO ANOTHER character from one of Woolf's novels, Peter Walsh, who's getting ready for Clarissa Dalloway's party in *Mrs. Dalloway*. Peter has a problem a lot of us have: He's sometimes bored by the monologue in his head. Or he's unsatisfied with it. He likes himself, but is often lonely and would love someone to keep him company through big decisions. He almost wants a second consciousness to sit inside his head through his crossroads—to laugh and feel with him, to know his private moments.

· · · · ·

HE DOESN'T LOVE BEING an individual. Now he paces in his hotel room, buttoning his shirt, searching for his wallet, getting ready to head out, alone on his London walk to Clarissa's party. He's fifty-three and has really come to town to get Clarissa's word about a woman who's soon to be his fiancée. He's in love with this much younger woman, and isn't sure if his choice is right. He worries that he hasn't *ever* made the right decisions, that people don't really like him.

· · · · ·

HE'S TRAVELED A LOT, but he thinks the memories would sparkle more if Clarissa had also seen the places he'd been. I know this feeling: He thinks the trip gets richer when presented to someone else. You take out photos from a trip and show them to friends. As familiar faces shuffle through your glossies, your emotions grow: The scattered details from the trip coalesce into a better story. As your friend sees your hotel room in Albuquerque, your memory feels more and more solid. That old hotel room now feels more like the setting of a juicy scene, the place you made choices and changed.

The trip was also fun as it happened, but even then, the greatest moments were dotted with anticipation of telling them to someone else. Stories always get their meaning by being told. A hike is just a series of moments until it's put into a story, and then we can hear what the *point* is. That's not just a truth about the "stories" of our vacations or about connections in Virginia's books, but the basis of literature itself. We give anything meaning by framing it—in a book, a letter, or narrated slide show—to pass it to another person who's not exactly like you, but works to imagine your experience.

Each moment in Albuquerque gains meaning because

of its relation to people you know. You're in a boring part of town but want to make it memorable, so the wig store next to your hotel becomes a hot spot, a joke, because your brother wore a big blond wig last weekend to your costume party. Your lover loves burritos, and that fact helps you decide what to eat on the last night of the trip: A local Mexican restaurant now looks more meaningful than the consumer chain it is. Sometimes, just the memory of what we share makes something sweet. When my colleagues went to the San Francisco Jazz Festival, they fell in love with the trumpeter Jim Rotondi. They came back to work ecstatic about the shared discovery. They're partly still such avid fans because they hit upon this music together. Communication sets the frame for what feels right.

· · · · ·

THE PHENOMENON THERE, WHICH Woolf could describe so well, is common enough. We feel attached to activities when they're part of a meaningful community. This is part of the reason, for instance, why a whole generation of kids has come to enjoy reading itself since discovering *Harry Potter*. It's not just the fact that the series is better than other children's books in the past few decades (though they are good); it's also because reading communities have developed around the books. I've seen a local

TV show where kids come on to compete in Potter trivia. *How many goal posts are there on a Quidditch pitch? What color was the sweater Harry got for Christmas?* The game connects the people involved, so these kids have a relationship to the books that is supported by actual people.

· · · · ·

PSYCHOLOGISTS WOULD LOOK AT what's called "internalizing" a voice here. The idea is that we learn both our values and how to separate from those who teach us by internalizing voices around us. I learn how to deal with certain situations by watching, and echoing, the way other people around me have done it. The Potter trivia show TV host, for example, becomes an internalized voice that applauds, and so encourages, a kid's ability to read. The contestants are also a community that supports the group's activity.

Internalized voices are comforting because they give assurance about what's valuable and worth choosing. They're a stabilizing presence that know, and partly form, who we are. Parents supply the central internal voice for most of us, and those who believe in God get the most dependable inner voice through Him, because He determines what's right, supplies those choices with their innate value, and monitors your progress toward a universal goal.

Because Woolf didn't think a traditional or observing God existed, maturity in her world meant suffering a bigger sense of isolation when you make big decisions. Our internalized parents, teachers, friends, and lovers give the sound of what matters: why people care; how *they* would act in different situations; what's valued. But these words of comfort and advice are only ever slices of the human character in Woolf, which means that ten competing opinions can mount to a clatter in your head that doesn't hide, but is all you've got of, the truth. Being independent means dealing with these competing ideas, making contact with these people who matter to you, but then stomaching the ambivalence in carving out your own choice—which is likely to be an opinion that no other head in the world *completely* hears or agrees with. We join each other in memories, but, when alone, we sort through the echoing voices on our own.

When Woolf rewrites the traditional model of God's intimacy with you, she replaces the celestial face with the overarching voice of human chatter, the gossip that sets our standards, links us, and even continues to sound over the Earth after the death of individuals. She presents her best image of this crest in the sky when she flies a plane over London in the novel *Mrs. Dalloway*, and all her characters, scattered through London, look up to see it. The plane putters out an advertising message in smoke letters, and as everyone watches the letters unfold, each focuses on the same thing but reaches a slightly different idea of what the plane's spelling. One man reads one word; another person, on the other side of town, sees the same three letters and decides the plane's spelling something else. After time, and to a limited extent, the scattered heads reach similar conclusions. But some might go off to lunch and miss the end of the plane's sentence. Some might lose interest. Some might misread. The point is that our communication links us, and if someone could rise above Earth, she would hear this ongoing conversation, which rises from our books, our advertising companies, and our computers and movies. But while connection rises, we also sort through it in heads that are distinct from one another. No one interprets the plane's message in the sky—or a line in a book or a conversation—*exactly* as I do. So in Woolf, being myself means dealing with this feeling of isolation, the nearly divine seclusion with the sounds inside.

In essence, this means the strongest people in Woolf can listen to friends and guides but are also good at stomaching the solitude with which we make decisions. Big decisions largely happen in private places like the hotel room her character Peter is pacing; and as time passes, we're the only ones who handle whatever comes from our choices. Woolf is interested in solitude: what it feels like, how it compares to company, and how to deal with its seeming flatness or ambiguity when no other voice structures the dialogue. She warns us that solitude is "divinely beautiful [and] also divinely heartless," in the essay "On Being Ill." "Human beings do not go hand in hand the whole stretch of the way. . . . Here we go alone." Sometimes friends "console not by their thought of us but by their forgetfulness," which means I remember what friends have said, and enjoy the miraculous memory of their concern, but then move around my room by myself.

· · · · ·

I KNOW MY OWN desire for company, because when I make a decision, my first impulse is often to call a friend. It's as if my decision has less meaning if not reported to someone who agrees with my choices. Someone's input also gives a sense of objectivity. My choice is arbitrary in the sense that it always could have gone another way. Checking in with someone else can, for whatever reason, make my course feel more natural or necessary. Woolf says that comfort has a lot to do with simply replacing silence by laughter and echo: "In the rough and tumble of daily life, [with friends] one had . . . a sense of repetition . . . so setting up an echo . . . full of vibrations," and so company lends anyone sweet reassurance in *To the Lighthouse*.

• • • • •

So: See Woolf's Peter struggle with solitude as he continues getting ready for the party and can't stop thinking of his friends. He doesn't want to marry someone without checking in with those who know him, which is his hunt for an "echo . . . full of vibrations."

As he finishes dressing, he plays a game you probably know—seeing himself as a player in his friends' eyes. He buttons his cuff and looks in the mirror imagining himself to be *the guy they know, Peter*. He's *that guy*, he thinks, as he sorts through his wallet—*their Pete, who will get married and one day retire to do research in the British Library*. His identity sinks into whatever outside stories they have about him.

• • • • •

In parallel in history, in a 1920 diary, my grandfather recorded a childhood fantasy rooted in the same desire. Until about age ten, my grandfather said, he believed God was his audience ("He chose to focus on me, I thought, among billions," my grandfather wrote). He thought God observed every move he made, as if the Lord sat on his shoulder at the toilet, while he was getting ready for school, walking home. Constant company was his security blanket through childhood, he wrote.

Who doesn't want a second opinion, especially if it

means confirmation? Peter nestles in the warm feeling of the eagle's eye. He draws relationships close.

The Big But

But the point is that Woolf wants to direct us to the flip side, too—to see that complete intimacy is a fantasy, and to know why a sense of belonging to others can even be a little cramping.

As an exercise here, imagine Peter finally getting out of that hotel and going to Clarissa's party. In Woolf's book, the following scene doesn't happen just like this, but I'm tailoring it in order to press harder on the personality Woolf herself crafted in Peter Walsh. Imagine that Peter walks into the party, waves hello to someone, and goes over to the wine table—where, to his great surprise, he runs into his boss. Peter depends on his boss's approval, too, and it's tricky here because the boss is an unknown player of sorts. The personal distance can make Peter nervous. *What does he see when he looks at me?* Peter wonders.

The boss makes small talk, wipes his lips, then drops a bomb, which is really just a casual comment about their work. "Pete, you've got to be on time more," he says. Peter stares, swallows, says he'll try to be. The two go to different parts of the room. Blurring his eyes out the window, sipping wine, Peter pretends to look nonchalant, but he's not. His boss's comment stays with him, lands on his shoulder like "a central oyster of perceptiveness, an enormous eye," as Woolf describes the feeling of presence in her essay "Street Haunting: A London Adventure."

As Peter drinks and listens to party buzz, he inflates perspectives, wondering if his boss had been thinking of Peter as lazy for this whole time. Had there been office conversations about his habits? A guy used to pleasing others, Peter thinks his professionalized routine might be a water cooler theme among others in the office.

This isn't real paranoia on Peter's part, but an inability to unravel his own concern with himself from his boss's experience in the world. He's collapsed his world and his boss's, as if what concerns Peter most (his own image) concerns his boss in the same way.

Woolf warns us that memories of others will trail us like strings: You'll feel "one's friends were attached to one's body, after lunching with them, by a thin thread," in *Mrs. Dalloway*. That is: You have a hard time untwisting your string and a friend's, who after lunch has actually moved on to a new activity you don't know about. The problem with Peter is that he hasn't realized that the boss doesn't think of Peter all the time—that he's less invested in picking Peter apart than Peter is. If Peter were able to recognize this difference in perspective—that the boss is living in his own world, in which Peter is a semi-important staff member but *not* the main character—Peter might be able to breathe deeper and make decisions with less weight on his shoulders. Choose to be on time or not. Marry or not. Who else is going to sit through the aftermath of it all like you will?

Seeing differences in perspectives is a letting-go filled with anxiety and joy. Lily in *To the Lighthouse* shudders to experience "violently two opposite things at the same time; that's what you feel, was one; that's what I feel, was the other, and then they fought together in her mind . . . so beautiful, so exciting, this love."

True: beautiful. My closest friends are the ones I go to for input, my backdrop theme song. But life also gets more potent when I see I'm hallucinating anyone's constant presence. At some point in life, the lover's away, mom's gone, and the fantasy of the oyster's eye is unmasked as a hallucination of security. I'll be late. I'll marry. I'll tell my friends but race through history on my own.

Although no writer I know gave more glory to the relationships and memories that bind us, Woolf also directs us to autonomy, to our creativity in hanging out in hotels, in winning or ditching *Harry Potter* contests, in being late, in deciding what parts of the vacation to talk about.

I Change

To understand Woolf's "so beautiful, so exciting, this love" description of autonomy, we need to understand some things about her. Her mother died when she was thirteen; her sister Stella when she was fifteen; her father when she was twenty-two; her brother Thoby when she was twenty-four. One sister, Laura, was mentally ill and sent away when Virginia was five. This means she was highly attuned to loss, memory, and the way thoughts of friends play out in your solitude.

Woolf sees the loneliness in crowds, asking why we never get to fully know our friends, even when they live right next to us. She's fascinated with the pecking game—in which we stare at each other, learn what we can as we do, and then move past on our natural cycle, with limited information. We only get pieces of our closest friends. Understanding the distance is fundamental for feeling fine about the gaps.

One reason you don't fully know people is that they're always changing. If there is a still center, we're too various with each other to see it. Woolf's characters often feel a desire to dig their hooks into people they're speaking to, but usually feel like they sink deep in dizzying waters as they try. A character facing a friend in the novel *The Years* feels like he's "sinking; he was falling under [the] weight"— and that's typical. Most characters suffer nausea when they recognize that knowing is an incomplete process, overloaded by ever-changing personalities.

Woolf takes us through the process of getting to know anyone by enacting Lily's perspective in *To the Lighthouse*, when Lily imagines an old friend, Paul, and wrestles with what she can actually grasp of him: "[So this] is what we call 'knowing' people, 'thinking' of them, 'being fond' of them!" she sighs. *What do I know of Paul?* To conjure up his identity, you have to pick out old memories and stitch them together. Think of your friend Paul. You once saw him fixing a tire. You once saw him fight with his girlfriend on the stairs of their house. These individual memories bob in your head. He stands in front of you and *seems* to solidly exist, but "knowing" anyone is 99.9 percent recall, which you largely edit or make up.

That's about as close as we get, and the made-up material in "knowing" fascinated Woolf. She adds to this model the fact that the personality adapts to shifting contexts. " 'You' and 'I' and 'she' pass and vanish; nothing stays; all changes," she writes in *To the Lighthouse*. Paul is a more formal person with his boss, a more open person with his wife, a simpler person with kids. Getting to know Paul would mean confronting him from one of these perspectives.

Woolf was fascinated with her own capacity to change. On August 22, 1922, she was writing in her diary in her room, and a friend knocked at the door. She had to look up, she wrote, and snap into an appropriate pose for that particular friend. She resented the need to become a singularly recognizable "Virginia." In the middle of her writing, "Sydney comes in & I'm Virginia," she recalled in her diary, and "when I write I'm merely a sensibility. Sometimes I like being Virginia, but only when I'm scattered & various & gregarious." She felt full of potential, and felt as if those shavings were magnetized in just one, nearly arbitrary way when her friend knocked on her door to see "Virginia."

• • • • •

WOOLF EXTENDS THE IDEA of your distance from others through Lily's eyes again in *To the Lighthouse*. Woolf builds a new metaphor here, saying knowing anyone is also like forming her image, painting her portrait. Lily is a painter in the novel who spends most of the book out in a field, trying to paint an actual, accurate picture of Mrs. Ramsay, whom she loves. Mrs. Ramsay's posing in her porch chair. For hours at a time, Lily struggles away at her easel, trying to put the image of the lady out there onto the canvas. But she's frustrated that she can't be what we'd call a typical realist. She's jealous of some idea of realism— that another artist would capture all of Mrs. Ramsay as she objectively, eternally *is*. Lily's locked into a style: Every mark she makes includes some of what her own personality adds. She's prone to certain stylistic twitches and to certain colors; who she *is* affects how she sees and thinks of others.

She struggles for objective realism as a painter. But then halfway through the book, Woolf kills Mrs. Ramsay off. After ten years pass, Lily goes back to the field to try to paint from memory. Now she finds some peace with how relationships work: You always insert parts of yourself. There's no such thing as fully decoding another person, and intimacy involves the way two personalities affect each other. What's more, time plays a role. You only know the sides of your friend that you happened to see. From scattered details, you invented a whole.

The places you've been and the moments you've enjoyed define the boundaries in how you know a friend. You pull up memories; you collect them together; and you only get that side of your friend that the friend assumed with you. In turn, Woolf says we only find calm in intimacy when we know that people don't boil down to something fixed and specific.

Think of the feeling of solitude. To have a memory of some joint vacation, and to call a friend and bug and bug her until she remembers it just like you do—to pry until you think the same—is more cloying than connecting. Lily finally understands this fact: that you'll sometimes live with a different memory or idea than your friend does, and that living well with each other means weathering your differences as well as the ways you mirror each other. Mrs. Ramsay has died, which forces Lily to surrender knowing some things about the friend who lived. She's got to paint this portrait now on her own, with the information she's got. When she does accept the boundaries in knowing, the relationship feels lighter. She's not going to fully encompass Mrs. Ramsay; she's going to half-create her; but that's all "knowing" is. She puts her brush to the canvas, and lets herself even project a little—to simply evoke this friend. She "drew a line there, in the centre," Woolf writes. "It was done; it was finished. Yes, she thought, laying down her brush in extreme fatigue, I have had my vision." The vision is about accepting your limited but heartfelt role in your relationships.

· · · · ·

THIS IDEA CARRIES MOST force in family situations, which can be the most delicate in an effort to know someone. If we know anyone at all, we're supposed to know family. But the ache to know can often stiffen so much that it causes tension. Imagine this scenario: A mother is passing by her teenage daughter's bedroom and stops in the shadows. Her daughter's feet are up on the wall and, unaware of her mother there, she talks on the phone: "Oh my God, she's a total *F. An A.P.L.*"

Mom doesn't know what the letters mean. She's dying to know—feels like she and her daughter have so much squaring up to do. Their own conversations have often been good, but Mom also hurts a little when she sees her daughter in such an *unfamiliar* but happy pose.

The mother might want to know her daughter's life from all its angles, but insistent prying would be more frustrating than helpful here. When Lily's desperate to *know* Mrs. Ramsay, she wants "fifty pairs of eyes to see with. [But] fifty pairs of eyes were not enough to get round that one woman." Woolf suggests it's best to get to a trusting place in which you allow your partner to have some secrets. The mom here needs to learn just enough to trust her daughter's choices, and then let the infinite small details go.

It's ugly to pin someone down with a prying insistence on mundane facts. Relationships have more grace when the fist relaxes. "The pin [that needs specificity] had something to do with one's own impotency," Woolf writes in an essay, "Evening Over Sussex: Reflections in a Motor Car." Throughout her work, she disparages an obsessive nailing-down.

· · · · ·

MY FRIEND RECENTLY GAVE me parallel advice with this: "Let them *come to you* more. Stop chasing. It's exhausting and unattractive."

· · · · ·

THE IDEA, FOR WOOLF, is that some things keep other people a mystery. One is that there's no "core" to pin down and possess. The corollary is that you and I are always changing, offering different styles of presentation to each other, pursuing different things from time to time. With no rigid core, our personalities shift.

Woolf says we've got to trust in a communication between these changeling selves that is just *good enough* to get a solid "identity" across. Too much insistence shows a lack of balance. Woolf loves a relationship that honors our tendency to morph; she also loves a personality that can stand relatively calm with its solitude.

Science Calls Your Changes Health

Two studies in science give Woolf's idea of allowing change good support here. Woolf was writing that we've got to let personalities change, unrecorded, with time. Science research best echoes the idea in a 1969 study, in which the psychologist Walter Mischel published a controversial paper arguing that our personalities are less consistent than science had always claimed. In "Continuity and Change in Personality," he argued that context radically and routinely recasts us. In detailed subsequent studies, he gave personality tests to subjects, scoring them in terms of traits like "extraversion" and "agreeableness." He then went on to show that the participants only performed those personality traits in a small percentage of the contexts they entered. His study was evidence that context is more powerful than we often admit. You're not going to look consistently shy, or demanding, or aggressive in different situations. Mischel ended up developing his work into a complex formula about how personality shifts in its context, but his basic idea has stayed the same throughout his career: On a statistical level, you're simply not the same amount of "shy" or "generous" around different crowds. You adapt to play roles depending on the other characters in the room. Woolf said this neatly in a letter to her friend Ethel Smyth in 1937. "The soul," she wrote, is like "those scraps of colour in a funnel [kaleidoscope] that we played with as children." It shifts its design depending on whose hands it's in.

Point number two, from science: If you allow yourself to play out different roles with different people, then this could be a nice sign of health. James Pennebaker and R. Sherlock Campbell study the way we heal ourselves through writing. In one study, they asked their subjects to write on different topics from day to day. What they found was that those people who let themselves use radically different writing voices in different assignments—shifting, say, from a passage all written in the pronoun "I" to a third-person fictional story the next day—showed greater health gains during the time of the experiment. The psychologists concluded that playing games from time to time—assuming different voices, acting out different modes of being "me"— is an essential element to being healthy.

The message Woolf offers gets a nod in clinical research: Your friends will change in different environments, and you'll never know all of their moods and sides. The ache for full revelation is a source of frustration, and annoying to both sides. Our personalities want the room to shift. In the end, getting comfortable with that dance is also finding peace in independence.

CHAPTER 3

Shut Down

AFTER HER PARENTS DIED, Virginia's life gained some sadly tainted independence, and she moved to the Bloomsbury section of London with her brothers and sisters. They gathered a group of intellectual friends who would later be called the Bloomsbury Group. Just before turning thirty, she fell in love and then married Leonard Woolf, one of her brother's intellectual, quiet friends. Leonard—a skinny, tall Jew with a nervous tremor—had been managing the British colonies in Ceylon but came back to London to marry Virginia; soon they set up their own home.

Virginia never lost her attraction to those London parties of her childhood, where snobbery mixed with dependence. (Here's excitement rolling through her diary after a party at 46 Gordon Square in 1923: "Suppose one's normal pulse to be 70; in five minutes it was 120; & the blood, not the sticky whitish fluid of daytime but brilliant & prickling like champagne. . . . We collided, when we met: went pop . . . flattered, praised, and thought (or I did) of Shakespeare. . . . A great relish for the actual things—whatever they may be—old plays, girls, boys, Proust, Handel sung by [a friend].")

Going out in London was magic, if a bit of a risk. It rattled her nerves. Her husband, Leonard, wrote that Virginia was extraordinarily "sensitive to the actual mental and physical excitement of the party itself. . . . Sometimes, of course, owing to her peculiar vulnerability to the mildest slings and arrows of (not very) outrageous fortune, she would leave a boring party in despair as if it were the last scene of Wagner's Götterdämmerung with [our] House and the universe falling in flames and ruin about her ears."

So she felt ambivalence from high sensibility. Still, making her way around social circles was a source of learning for Virginia, and she always stayed curious. She would talk with friends and smoke late into the night, often venturing out without Leonard, who liked the drama of company less than she did. She was known for her chiseled, smart face, her white cotton dresses, her laugh, her cigarettes.

As she made her way through Bloomsbury, Soho, and Chelsea, one question about psychology that continued to fascinate Virginia was the way we shift between an open demeanor and a cold shoulder, or between confession and quiet. In essence: She came to acknowledge the occasional cold shoulder as a basic human defense. You can partly read this as her Victorian sensibility. Virginia knew some things needed to be kept inside, and she claimed that privacy was a valuable space.

She was in a torn position. On one hand, she understood the last generation's Victorian ethic: It's your right—even often charismatic—to have a private world of your own. On the other, she was a Modernist, and wanted to set the stage for open, spontaneous talk. She valued both her parents' silence and a bolder exposure.

Her appreciation of two worlds tells us something about ourselves—because if we switch to today, we see a massive shift to the modern side, to brazen forward motion. We're not as good with patience and calm—so that on our political talk shows, bold assertions pass as insight; on reality TV, audacity earns the spotlight; and CEOs consolidate their power by butchering self-doubt. Woolf would call this lust for the unambiguous a knee-jerk reaction to the past, and partly a mistake. Modern audacity can get dangerous when it devalues difference, or diminishes our right to nuanced thinking. In turn Woolf suggests why—however much you hate the "prude"—it's still worthwhile to give each other space from time to time, or to find our solitude, which can be a place for complex thinking.

Escape the Clatter

Virginia asked about our right to close down when she wrote about a famous London socialite Sybil Colefax in her essay "Am I a Snob?" Sybil hosted fashionable artists' lunches at her Argyll House in Chelsea, where local lights like Woolf, Arnold Bennett, and Noel Coward mingled. Virginia was first cynical of the superficiality of these parties, resenting Sybil's arrogance, her pride in having famous friends. But sometimes Virginia made her way over to the parties regardless.

Virginia actually made a memorable first entrance to Sybil's salon because on her first evening, she ran into Arnold Bennett after he'd knocked her novel *Orlando* in a review in the *Evening Standard*. She held her own with wit, saying, "You can't hate my books more than I hate yours, Mr. Bennett." Sybil loved the quip, and soon started inviting Virginia into her closer circle, for dinner, not just tea. They became better friends, so that Sybil also started visiting Virginia's less elegant house alone, sitting on the floor, eating burnt biscuits, and talking about her own loves, ambitions, and social fears. In her essay, Virginia wrote she'd struck gold—gotten past glossed exteriors to the beating heart of the hostess. She even enjoyed the deepening of that bond when Sybil's husband died, and Virginia became one of Sybil's closest confidantes.

· · · · ·

THE PROBLEM WITH THIS breakthrough authenticity was that it was short-lived. After a few weeks of mourning her husband, Sybil counteracted her soft bonding with Virginia by making a speedy return to the bold. She pulled an about-face—went back to her parties, dined out with other friends, rose from her depression by leaving Virginia behind in her own less glamorous surroundings. "I was not so well pleased . . . I was baffled," Virginia writes in her essay. She faced an old friend like facing an enigma. She couldn't understand Sybil's head: Had the woman been lying about her intimacy all along, or had she once really felt a connection, but changed interests?

· · · · ·

WORKING THROUGH THE QUESTION of a friend's coldness, Virginia brings our attention to a human fact: Victorian or modern—snob or genuine friend—we operate more like valves than open books. We can't, as modern trends might demand, *deliver everything quick and fast*. We hold a lot in—as complex minds who can't be bullied into consistent or simple appearances.

The reason it seemed like Sybil clammed up is that there were a couple of equally fundamental drives in Sybil Colefax. Sometimes she liked a party; sometimes she wanted to confess and cry on the floor with an introspective artist. For Virginia to grant the woman true humanity, she had to allow her her roaming perspective, without flattening it with a demand to *speak one thing*.

I range. I don't reveal it all to you, because I can't. Some of my interests make no sense to you. When I range, I sometimes look two-faced. The fact is—Virginia at her strongest would admit—not all sides of my head align with yours, and knowing I'm human means allowing for some non-communication between us.

Enter Woolf's essay "Evening over Sussex: Reflections in a Motor Car," in which she's riding in a car, down a road in southern England, watching the trees, a haystack, a roof, people walking with bags, and she's sunk in thought. Twilight soaks the evening, and it's too early for people to light their homes. Woolf sinks in the dim, bumps through silence; she'd rather her friend, the driver, not break the mood with small talk. "Sit and soak," Virginia writes in the essay. Be quiet. "Do not bother because nature has given you six little pocket knives with which to cut up the body of a whale," she writes. She means that anxious driving companions demand a quick dissection and description of the landscape. But that demand for conversation is sometimes just fear of how you think in silence. So, wait. Waiting has its own payoff.

You can see what she's saying by thinking of contemporary celebrities like Donald Trump or Bill O'Reilly whose shows are entertaining because they keep a darting pace and rate amplified, unapologetic thinking as the strongest type of analysis we can do. Woolf would read that bias for single-mindedness as a flavor of tyrannical thinking: a denial of the diversity that stages its challenge when you're less self-assured.

This is the same sort of warning we've had from modern thinkers like Archibald MacLeish, for instance, who wrote an article for *The Nation* reminding us of what's insidious about muscular American advertising speak. MacLeish wrote that we might use our shotgun commercial vocabulary well to sell things like cigarettes and Cokes, but if we try to rely on a fiery self-styling for selling democracy abroad, we've lost our sense of humanity. Dealing with real concepts like human rights means dropping the strong-arming language of TV or the advertising world to welcome the ambiguous in.

· · · · ·

WOOLF WANTS US TO admit the doubts native to any situation—or to sometimes slow down and shut up. Going slower means admitting difference—which sometimes means allowing other people autonomy in their viewpoints. I don't fully understand the person I'm negotiating with, and I shouldn't insist on full accord. Admitting variance between perspectives is central to getting along.

· · · · ·

WE CAN SEE SOME of that compromise between Woolf and Sybil. Virginia was hurt when Sybil recoiled from the role of confidante back to hardened socialite, but Woolf also knew it was moral to allow that woman to go. That is, it takes strength to grant a friend privacy and difference, or to sit still as she pursues her flock of hidden interests. Here's a test: If someone was once interesting to you but has since moved on, subdue your impulse to blame her for some total or damnable duplicity. I have to try to sit tight as I admit my former friends are complicated, that they range between interests, and that no interesting and lasting friend is utterly consistent.

Room for Thinking

In a poignant moment of her life, Virginia found space for her own thinking when she lied to a good friend. Right after Virginia moved to Bloomsbury with her siblings, they all took a vacation to Greece, meeting up with their family friend Violet Dickinson. On the trip, Virginia's brother Thoby caught typhoid, and when they got home, he died. Virginia was devastated, because she was closer to Thoby than almost anyone else in her life. But after the death—and because Violet was also sick—Virginia wrote Violet a month of letters in which she pretended Thoby was still alive and recovering.

On one hand, you can almost see insanity there—poor Virginia can't fully mourn yet, so she becomes practically schizophrenic with the projection of a dream reality. She hides her trauma from her friend. But you can also see something admissible in the evasiveness. She's doing something similar to the daydreaming she described in the Sussex driving essay: You're not obliged to say everything to the person next to you, because sometimes thoughts need space to process.

. . . . .

THINK OF HOW NATURALLY we operate like valves with one another. In a basic example, imagine a mother on line for a Disneyland ride with her two kids. The kids are bored, tugging on her shirt, already tuned into a truth: Mom holds things back. With boredom and time, the kids run with a fantasy: If they're loud and persistent enough, they might get Mom to crack, or to expose her whole interior. "Be honest, Mom!" one says. "If you had to kill just one of us, who would it be? Who do you love more? Just say it. We can take it. We won't get mad."

Mom is tired. Knowing communicating with people means modulating for kindness, not just truth, she won't spill all she thinks. She peels an orange, rolls her eyes, smiles as she drops a rind in the trash. "I love you equally."

. . . . .

IN THE SAME VEIN, women in Woolf's novels show their grace by holding some things back. The men in the books like to spout their facts and philosophies like dogma—fire from the gun, shot to awe and impress. The women know there's stuff they don't know, and stuff that's supposed to go unspoken, at least for a while—for the sake of kindness, depth, or difference. Woolf's quiet women are beautiful not just because they know a coy Victorian pose, but because they won't domineer the public space. Again, casting forward to today, Woolf would find the devil in Simon Cowell with his razor-sharp criticism on *American Idol*, or other TV hosts who thrive by shaming the weak. She describes these aggressive men, in *A Room of One's Own*, as "killing some . . . insect as [they talk], but even [killing it] did not satisfy him; he must go on killing it." The guy thinks violently asserting himself is the only way to gain respect. "Had he been laughed at, to adopt the Freudian theory, in his cradle by a pretty girl?" Woolf writes. Shut up for truth: "It is in our idleness," she goes on, "in our dreams, that the submerged truth sometimes comes to the top." So she warns us that dominance is usually a fear of deep thinking, anxiety about the opposing opinions you'd have to consider if you gave them a second of airtime.

· · · · ·

It's easy to find Woolf's love of the quiet voice alive in other parts of our modern life. Go to the utterly non-Victorian Bob Dylan, for instance. Dylan is a singer who rallied for self-expression but hated the bullying journalist's impulse to boil down life into a headline that could sell a paper. Whenever they used to try to pin him down, asking, *Mr. Dylan, how does it feel to be the "voice of a generation"?* he'd refuse that line of questioning. He'd put on that enigmatic smile that recapitulates Clarissa Dalloway's silence.

In an interview in March 1965, Dylan dodged the ugly onslaught. When a journalist asked him to define his "philosophy," he returned with his trademark elusive grin, and comedy: "Are you kidding? The world don't need me," he said. "Christ, I'm only five feet ten. The world could get along fine without me. Don'cha know, everybody dies. It don't matter how important you think you are. Look at Shakespeare, Napoleon, Edgar Allan Poe, for that matter. They are all dead, right?"

Dylan knew privacy was important when the public realm was asking for something simple. He didn't want to spend the energy to pump nuance back into the whole clichéd line of talk about his "generation." He would stick to music, let others define the era in prose if they wanted. That's an ethics of respecting individuals' opinions.

Think of Woolf's ride through the countryside: You don't demand accord with the person next to you, and no one needs to definitively rate the landscape. Your exploration of the world can happen at its own pace, unbullied, complex in quiet.

That's frustrating to the reporter. But it's precious fuel on a human level, Woolf would say. Our own contemporary impulse toward the unquestioned judgment or the headline is much more dangerous than it was in Woolf's own time, too. We inflate the heroism around our bullies— celebrities who capture the world by reducing ambiguity. Woolf says we need to sit with loose ends.

In her essay "How Should One Read a Book?" Woolf warns us against the hard exterior that's set to prove itself, like a cowboy taming the West, in which we "load and aim and shoot." Her point is that one of the most difficult tasks in being (always admittedly egotistical) humans is staying calm while difference happens—keeping a lid on our need to *stake* and *prove*. Silence is sometimes a fabulous strategy—a way to expand the head, and to be fair to people around you.

CHAPTER 4

Take on Challenging Friendships

MAKING HER WAY THROUGH party circles, Virginia was known as a wit. With this gift, she had a knack for building some fabulously memorable friendships. She liked people who could challenge her, engaging in a rivalry with Katherine Mansfield (the one woman she claimed jealousy of); an intellectual partnership with Lytton Strachey; and a social dance with Ottoline Morrell, whose Bedford Square parties intermittently disgusted and thrilled Virginia.

Woolf knew the discomforts of relationships, and her best friendships could be as prickly as they were warm. For

Virginia, comfort wasn't gold in life, especially if comfort meant stasis. Her bias for fire is shown in her most memorable loves, in which we'll see her test her sexuality, push her intellect, and endure jealousy. Relationships that push your buttons, she knew, can teach you something.

Manic Ethel

We get a true dose of how much she could dare in her friendship with Ethel Smyth, a composer who threatened to upset Woolf's comfortable routine. Ethel was seventy-two and Woolf forty-eight when they met. Ethel was practically Woolf's opposite: louder with her ambitions ("I am the most interesting person I know, and I don't care if anyone else thinks so," she claimed in 1935); a chubby and passionate lesbian; a publicly vocal suffragist. She was known to walk into a party with her dog before her, mud thick on her boots from a hunting trip. She liked tennis and golf, was a sloppy eater, a loud talker, and wore green and purple neckties to represent the colors of the fight for the woman's vote. She ended up in jail after throwing rocks at a politician's window. While in jail, she scrawled out a message on her underwear, hung that intimate sign from her railing, and—keeping time with her toothbrush—led her inmates in several rounds of a ballad she'd written for women.

All of which is to say she was more outgoing than Woolf was comfortable with, and facing Ethel was like facing the physical shape of some things Virginia had repressed. Here was half mirror image, half opposite.

Partly because the friendship started from Ethel's fan mail, partly because of the age gap and physical distance (the relationship largely happened in letters), Virginia jumped at the chance to try on a new persona here. She had the distance to risk new roles with a fellow artist who shared some ambitions Woolf admired but hadn't quite acted upon. In real life, Virginia was Quiet Writer and Wife. She and husband Leonard would rise around eight, write side by side till noon, walk, work again; and she'd take her evening milk to her own bedroom. With Ethel, Virginia allowed herself to embody a sexier spirit.

• • • • •

THE TWO WOMEN HAD a nonphysical but violent passion in which they tried on oppositional styles. Virginia would get daring, prod and push, in a letter like this: "Well, what are you doing?—inducing a large penis into a small hole?" Ethel would absorb that energy and write back, "I don't think I have ever cared for anyone more profoundly."

"For eighteen months I really thought of little else." Woolf would agree, saying Ethel thrilled her because she was "generous and free and fierce." In the hub of anonymity, they became new women.

But after trying on new voices and showing more emotion than normal, Virginia also felt the tug of the routine that always returns in the morning. Some shame could set in. That is, Virginia would play Diva one afternoon, and the next morning, she could remember her role as Leonard's serious wife; as reserved, well-known novelist, and enact a defensive spit in Ethel's face: "To the casual onlooker you seem exaggerated," she wrote, clinging to dignity one day in 1931. "I think [you are] the most attitudinising unreal woman I've ever known. . . . Why should I stand this manhandling, this brawling this bullying, this malusage? . . . Why cowtow to the bragging of a Brigadier Generals daughter?"

• • • • •

THE SWING BETWEEN ECSTASY and defensiveness remained extreme throughout the relationship; it's an instability that is recognizable. Tolstoy acknowledged that tension between new passion and resentment in *The Kreutzer Sonata*, in which he wrote, "periods of [love] were short, and generally followed by periods of irritation. . . . Irritation depended very regularly upon the periods of love . . . two opposite faces of the same animal feeling." Growth brings an irritating kickback. But all great historical romances tell us this. Fitzgerald almost ran over his wife, Zelda, on purpose; Charlie Chaplin satisfied his sex addiction through his career by marrying a string of sixteen-year-olds, only graduating to marrying an eighteen-year-old when he was fifty-four; Shakespeare was insensitive in leaving his wife his "second-best bed" in his will. Most big minds are uneven. Adventure means instability; it often means the swing from risk to regret.

I think all of us know this dynamic on a less magnified scale: Sometimes we get into a relationship with a new friend, and we might try something unusual. The start of something new excites us, and we are compelled to be a little bolder, louder, more playful. But after a rise on a high, the next moment can also trigger the stress of the split self. For me, if the old routine is set off balance, I can get moody and self-doubting.

The next step is often a need to run. Having some need to save face, I usually want to leave these tough connections.

Woolf would say the discomfort in dynamic relationships is unavoidable. If possible, *don't run*. She doesn't want to glorify our abusive ties, but Virginia does ask that we stop defining maturity—in yourself or your relationships—as an even temperament. Maturity is not the ability to keep calm. It's the willingness to face your reactivity.

My reactivity, or my acting out, is the spot where I've got the chance to see myself. Woolf would say that a need to look conventionally cool or mature inhibits our efforts to learn. She showed her own willingness to sit with herself in her relationship with Ethel—in which she would risk and recoil, but not let the potentially embarrassing tension break the friendship.

Here's the test she's giving: Am I the type of person who can admit I'm uneven or, better yet, feel shame? I was at the theater the other day, and a woman was asked to move her seat. She refused, stood, wrapped her shawl around her neck, and said she was a patron. "You're asking me to *move*? I fund this theater." People were snickering, because the drama seemed to have started without the play beginning. This woman *felt no shame* about her defensiveness. She didn't have the ability to think, "I'm being irrational. Why?" Her inability to introspect was probably the anchor for her pride, but it limited how accurately she could understand herself in the world. The ability to doubt yourself is a key to building and adjusting relationships.

Psychology values your willingness to sit with your mistakes. The psychologist W. Ray Crozier has studied shame and the human blush—even building a formula that equates shame with your ability to put yourself in someone else's shoes. In terms of relationships, this means admitting you're often erratic and mistaken; situations unsettle you, and you've got to accept you're imperfect—and then not run from the mess you make. If you can face, and stomach, your mistakes, you're closer to knowing the person you are with others. My ability to know that my conversation partners have different perspectives is a crucial step in understanding who I am outside of my own assumptions.

· · · · ·

VIRGINIA KNEW SHAME (SOMETIMES too much). One night she was so hot, and then so cold, she told Ethel she didn't like her. They were having some spat, and Virginia lashed out, saying, "I don't suppose I am really fond of anyone." Then she went home. That was a point at which—if shut down or too scared—she would have cut the relationship off to save face. She'd pretend she'd been *right*, not moody. But she didn't cut the relationship off. Within a few days, she opened her notebook, and wrote a letter to Ethel in which she went over the night and admitted her emotional volatility, acknowledging that she'd snapped because she'd felt defensive.

The too-proud or helplessly embarrassed types would run to deny their behavior. Virginia could admit her moods, and stuck with Ethel for years. She wasn't so vain that she needed to always look mature, but could admit embarrassment if it promised to teach her something. She let passions rattle, and knew herself in the range there.

Maturity, Woolf is saying, does not mean being utterly predictable. She isn't offering a ticket to be demanding with friends, but she does want us to admit our moods, to better know ourselves. If I pretend I'm always right—and always happy about it—I don't know myself. Woolf dared to expose her ranging emotions with Ethel. Although the trip wasn't easy, Woolf learned about herself here, and had a famous ride doing it, too.

Get Naked (in Personality or Body) to Build a Bond

The friendship with Ethel went on for ten years—and know it was not some isolated case of exploration for Virginia. She *liked* dynamic duos. Layer the picture by considering her more famous love affair with Vita Sackville-West.

These two actually did sleep together. They met in 1922, and started a sexual romance in 1925, on a visit to Vita's Long Barn house without their husbands.

Virginia was immediately awed stiff. Vita was a very wealthy, androgynous poet with a more adventurous sexual past than Virginia had had. Vita and her husband, Harold, had pursued open affairs, with one episode culminating in such passion that Harold had to chase his wife to France to beg her to come back.

Virginia met Vita through a friend, and initially it was a chaste connection made up of conversation and meals they shared together. It was during one winter weekend that Virginia got to Vita's house, passed a typical evening, but then sat on the bed and finally felt the chance of doing what was strange for her. They kissed. They spent three nights together. Each morning they started a routine that they'd revisit about a dozen times over the years—after a night of love and sleep, they'd read the newspaper in bed, sipping tea, then get ready for a walk on the downs, for playtime with Vita's sons.

Imagine what this situation felt like for the already well-established and bookish writer at forty-three, whose marriage was almost sexless at this point. Transpose the risk to life. You're sitting at a bar with a new friend who amazes you with her difference, but somehow you feel a basic trust. You see risk lying just over the horizon—a secret you could tell, a confession you could make.

You sit with tight lips—at a crossroads. You've got two

choices: to play it safe and have a nice drink and go home contented, or to let a bomb drop—some new word or even a kiss.

Of course there are reasons to not be the drama queen. You've lined up things well enough in your life. You're OK. No need to rip at the seams.

There are other reasons to step over the ledge and let loose that new idea or action.

If it's someone you trust, Virginia might say, try it. It means rolling the dice for a new type of connection. Before more of Virginia and Vita, think of *The Picture of Dorian Gray*, Oscar Wilde's novel in which a character can't be honest with friends. Dorian loves to risk when he's energized, but he keeps the adventures secret. A painting in his attic acts as the conduit for his life. The painting itself changes whenever Dorian acts on a passion; his own face never shows a wrinkle, so his friends never see any exterior sign of the risks he takes in private. Dorian feels empowered by his public purity for a while, but it finally amounts to an isolation in which he has no soulmate. When, in the end of the novel, he confronts his painting—himself—in the attic, the anxiety kills him.

Wilde's saying that you need to be authentic with another living person. Too strong a need for public polish can pervert you. Woolf's life would leave us with a similar message. Woolf let herself go with Vita. You can see it through the letters where the prudish Virginia confesses a ribald fantasy of seeing naked Vita stomping grapes in a vat, "stark naked, brown as a satyr, and very beautiful." Virginia gets giddy: *Love me*, she says, "[you] longeared owl and ass." She sings in these love notes, sometimes bearing the boldest and most vulnerable Virginia. The upshot was that the relationship became a rock at the center of her life.

You might hate how overused the word "soulmate" is, but this is the way you make one. A soulmate is the person who's gotten the chance to see something real about you. You risked; you bared ugliness; you forged a bond. This friendship becomes something more lasting than a superficial thing.

Soulmate means a friend who understands something about you and so lives flexibly in this relationship, in which you can both risk a little, and insult a little, and dare a little, and stray a little, while something solid connects you at the center.

• • • • •

INCREASINGLY, SOCIOLOGY HAS SHOWN that sharing secrets does do major work in increasing happiness with ourselves and trust with our confessors. In a study about how groups stay together, psychologists Gary Fine and Lori Holyfield identified two factors in cohesion: secrecy and trust. That is, groups stay together longest if they share some pressing insider information, and if they trust that the group members relate to and respect the information similarly. This truth about cohesion applies to our soulmates, too. Our bonds gain dependability when we share something with the power to unmask us. You'll find yourself with more dependable bonds if some risk happened in the formation of those bonds.

Psychology also comments on the health associated with honest confession. Rutger Engels, Catrin Finkenauer, and their research team, in studying children's relationships to their parents, found that—contrary to what you might assume—lying actually gives the experience of a *loss* in control. You try to master your life by keeping information from others, but you end up feeling frayed and frightened. That's something Oscar Wilde also implied when he had his all-too-private Dorian spin out of control with a mere illusion of a well-partitioned life.

· · · · ·

GIVEN THESE INSIGHTS INTO trust, we see what held Virginia and Vita together. They had risked, and so could always come back to each other with some stable understanding at the center. You see it near the end of their friendship. In 1938, Virginia published her political book *Three Guineas*, and Vita thought it was weak. "I wanted to exclaim, 'Oh, BUT, Virginia . . .' on about 50% of your pages," she wrote her in June 1938.

Virginia was hurt, and she spat back that Vita could never truly understand her. Should she have shown her the book at all? The women were at odds. They let their relationship cool for a while.

But a connection that had been formed through real exposure (the nights together, the talks, the sharing of writing throughout their lives) would bob back up. The sense of sisterhood withstood the spat. Here's Virginia on March 12, 1940. Vita's just asked if she should visit, and Woolf writes back to her, embracing her lover in the third person: "As for myself, I *never* feel out of touch with Vita. Thats odd but true. . . . For you'll never shake me off—no. not for a moment do I feel ever less attached. Aint it odd? [So] yes, do, do come [to visit]."

• • • • •

I BELIEVE THAT THERE are some friends you can call your friends even after there's been substantial spatial or emotional distance. They're internalized voices, so in some sense, they're inseparable from yourself. From my personal experience, I know these can be tense relationships. Sometimes I need to yell and get away from them, for years. But these friends color my memories and sense of self. What you've shared are the most meaningful memories you've got. After the air settles, these people are also the ones who understand your obsessions or humor.

· · · · ·

TOUGH FRIENDSHIPS, WOOLF WOULD say, are worth the energy. Risk is a little trauma with a big potential reward. You value some anger and shame because of its lessons. So Virginia found love in uncomfortable spaces, and her commitment to the often-bruising search repaid her.

CHAPTER 5

Find Steady Support

So far I've been stressing Virginia's excitement in imperfect and erratic relationships, but I might be overplaying that rebellious energy. After all, nothing was as important to her as maintaining a still point in the center—a place to work and feel respectable doing it. She chose to build her home with a husband—to keep a steady routine with reliable interpersonal support. Of course she married Leonard Woolf at thirty because she loved him, but the biggest payoff was probably having a dependable habit with a voice in her court whispering *you're worth it.*

Her marriage has sometimes been comfort for me as

I've thought of choices in my own life. You must get that pulse—you've committed to someone solid but occasionally ask what you're missing. I consider cutting all ties, because an absence of ties seems like it could mean a bigger life. Other days, you know that the heaven of freedom is only imagined. You weigh the rewards of relationships against the open air of independence.

At least in her choices, Virginia shows we're strongest when we keep at least one partner in our lives who stands behind us. We're biggest when we have a partner cheering us on, telling us to risk, accepting us even when we don't immediately make it.

Loving Calm

Leonard worked to establish their steady life before they got married, consulting Virginia's doctors about how best to care for her mood disorder. They set a plan: steady work that would lighten up when she got ill; milk before bed; good exercise and meals. They would often take long walks, and kept to a steady morning writing schedule.

Leonard's real gift was giving Virginia the feeling that one other person was completely in her court. Know this feeling: Imagine the difference between going to work in the morning when you do, versus when you don't, rattle with the voice of a friend or lover telling you *you're more intelligent than other people; no matter what they tell you, you're generous and interesting*. Again: Imagine the feeling of returning to your desk at work after a boss gives you a vote of confidence: *You're the best mind we have in this place.* The difference between living in the cradle of support and not having it can be the difference between working boldly and falling apart at the seams.

Science even says that you do better when you've got supportive input. Evidence comes in psychologist Barbara Fredrickson's "broaden-and-build theory" from 1998, which proved that people who experience positive emotions, like approval from a spouse, experience a momentary growth of what Fredrickson named "thought-action repertoires." Her research looks at how the mind actually shifts to a different register after being encouraged by external voices. In one interesting study, Fredrickson showed a variety of films to subjects, from angry to neutral to joyful films. After watching one of them, participants were asked to write twenty lines following the prompt "I would like to. . . ." The people who saw the positive films listed more things they'd think of doing than those who saw the negatively charged films did, and their choices covered a broader range, including more social and inventive activities.

Fredrickson, along with other researchers like Alice Isen, has run other tests to clarify just how the mind expands the range of what it considers or witnesses in the moments directly after it's been cradled with an optimistic message.

· · · · ·

THE IDEA IS THAT positive feedback doesn't only feel good, but actually changes your creative observation. After being told *you're good*, you are likely to switch energy from defensiveness to a broader range of possibilities.

We don't need to resort to formal psychology to understand the effects of support, which we can see pan out in some scenes from Virginia and Leonard's actual life together. One of the nicest things about their relationship was the way they respected their differences. She was more expressive and emotional than he was. Some critics say Virginia actually modeled the utterly cold Mr. Ramsay on Leonard, in contrast to her own emotional personality. She sometimes saw Leonard as a detached mind she could emulate but never be, as she mutters in her diary on December 2, 1939: "L. has trained himself to cut adrift . . . feelings. . . . L. very subtle & wise." But he wasn't exactly cold. He was a rational post-Victorian man who took careful steps to support Virginia. He was also intensely reflective, and certainly as accepting of their differences as she was. He pays respects in his autobiography, written after Virginia's death: "I have known people who [are] the 'sillies' whom Tolstoy thought were the best people in the world. There was something of the 'silly' in Virginia, as I always told her and she agreed. . . . Obviously there is something remarkably good in these streaks. . . . I am afraid there was never the touch of the 'silly' in me."

He knew how different they were. But he made it clear to her that he appreciated the difference, and his choices showed their connection. He often put his work aside to support Virginia. Leonard bought the Hogarth printing press to give her a stabilizing hobby in between her bouts of writing. He described her style elsewhere in his autobiography, enjoying "her attitude to her work, her art, her books. The vast majority of people work for about eight hours a day. . . . Virginia normally 'worked' 15 hours and I should guess that she dreamed about it most of the time when she was asleep. [When] writing, her concentration was 100, not 50, per cent."

Some marriages would crumble with this setup. These were two intellectuals with different styles. She liked emotional books; he was a more rational-minded politician. But they had a supportive give-and-take that worked.

Good marriages, they show, are mutual admiration

societies. Two people with different sensibilities respect those differences and even applaud the different roads they take. For Virginia, Leonard was the voice that says *I know and enjoy you*. Virginia could be terribly erratic, but she kept Leonard in her life because he was a stabilizing interior *yes*. See this small scene: One day in the late 1920s, Virginia and Leonard were visiting Vita, and they were all loading the car to go on a picnic. Vita's kids were loading into the back, and they were probably all packing the trunk with fruits and books and blankets to lay out. Virginia felt slightly overloaded by the commotion. She was also thinking of a book she was writing. But the kids were full of laughter, piling everything in, slapping each other, joking. Virginia wanted to join in but also felt her need for distance. Her eyes fazed out on the car. Suddenly she asked if they'd all mind if she just walked. It was six miles to their picnic stop. The question was odd—almost annoying. The kids rolled their eyes—*our crazy Aunt Virginia*. But Leonard leaned in and said of course she could walk.

In some ways, that's not a great picture of health. You'd want our heroine to feel less overwhelmed—to get over herself, to get in the loud, chaotic car and just enjoy it. But the nice part of this story is that Virginia kept people in her life who accepted various sides of her, who knew who she was, and didn't blame her for it. We also see Leonard's trust: He knew she wouldn't break down right then. He knew what she needed—to work through a mood with a six-mile walk. He didn't call her crazy for it. He gave her the room she requested, comforting her by really knowing and enjoying her.

·····

A MIRROR LIKE THAT matters. Virginia struggled with crippling depressions throughout her life but said she could not have found the guts to write what she did without a partner's support. Leonard routinely made her feel lighter, as the living counterpart to her depths. He's a buoy in her diary, in which she'll sink into her literary dream but then resurface to look at him: "L. is now reading" (February 3, 1938), she writes. "L. writing his play" (March 31, 1938). "L. now looking for water for Sally [their dog]" (June 16, 1938). "L. is writing in his garage room" (August 4, 1938). "L. has a sore throat this morning" (March 29, 1936). "Two days ago L. had the brilliant idea of converting half the library into an open air verandah with glass doors, in which we can sit on a hot night & survey the stars" (August 4, 1938).

"L" is the body who gives immediacy to her life, by fixing food, reading in the cushy chair, petting the dog, gardening. That's what a friend is: an external tie to love, to fun, to action. Leonard was a stabilizing force.

· · · · ·

MOST IMPORTANT, AS FREDRICKSON says in science, keeping a constant friend expands those "thought-action repertoires"—the range of possibilities you see at any one time. Woolf often claimed, and I'm willing to accept, that she often felt the effect of this momentary creative expansion.

Know something about Virginia's fiction: Its beauty is often its scope, the way it connects one character with another to make a large network of their viewpoints; she'll float above a city, through time, to show the pattern of human contact. When at its best, her talent shows itself in these sweeping moves. She's always excellent on the small details of the mind, but her work gains balance when she also steps back to link characters in a bigger picture.

Carry this idea back to the scientist Fredrickson, to another study on how pleasure affects brain activity. Fredrickson once gave images printed on cards to subjects, asking the participants to match one card with its mate. The cards could have been matched in two ways—through an irrelevant but exact detail that existed in some of them, or by a more meaningful global resemblance. Fredrickson found that depressed—read: lonely, unsupported—subjects tended to match cards by the nitpicky insignificant detail. Happier—supported, stable—subjects matched cards according to the larger thematic similarities. Again, she's talking about "broaden-and-build": that the mind gets relaxed and builds meaning better when it's given positive feedback. Frustrated minds tend to fixate on less significant details, perhaps in a struggle for control. They lack the sense of play to swing past small details to something widely meaningful.

That fact's sweet for me to remember, because I know it viscerally in my own work. I often imagine I work best when I cut off all ties to people and dig into my writing. Sometimes that route is best, for a while. But I almost always lose perspective when I shut down like that. When I have an outside partner in my life who takes me away and reminds me I'm fun or potent, I then go back to the work with a lighter touch, better balance in putting pieces in their places and creating a playful whole.

The message is especially salient with Virginia—a writer who often suffered with a closed-down depression, and whose specialty was the fine (some said insignificant) details of the mind. I do think her work is best when it balances that fine-tuned magnification work with the broader sweep, the playful line that comes from a woman's sense of validation. I sometimes make the quick comparison with Franz Kafka, who suffered a depression somewhat like Woolf's, with an ascetic's aversion to eating, a tendency toward solitude, and a pervasive darkness in his prose. But unlike Woolf, Kafka resisted marriage or any lifetime companion because he thought a relationship would hurt his art. Perhaps "the best mode of life for me would be to sit in the innermost room of a spacious locked cellar with my writing things and a lamp," Kafka wrote to his fiancée on January 14, 1913, before canceling the marriage plans, to write in a life without her. In turn—in comparison to Woolf's work—Kafka's stories are markedly claustrophobic, developing absurdities in an anorexic prose that's distinct but not an especially affirming read. For me, Woolf's writing wins out in the comparison: She has her eye on small details, dark spots, and absurdities, but is able to frame those observations in a more sociable human lens. Her work proves it can be a boost to have a partner who reminds us of the larger picture—who relaxes our attention and introduces play, who affirms our work is creative.

CHAPTER 6

Work Hard, Even Without a Sign of Success

VIRGINIA HAD A FANTASTICALLY frustrated time as a writer, and one big problem for her was the critics. She liked to tell herself they didn't matter, but she always struggled with what they got and didn't get in her books.

October 1924: The critic Frank Swinnerton writes in *Bookman* that Woolf is a "sterile . . . refined and pernickety" writer who can't figure out "what the devil to write about." October 9, 1931, in *Evening News*, Swinnerton again: Virginia publishes "bloodless" novels "approaching mush." June 6, 1925, from P. C. Kennedy in *New Statesman*: *Mrs. Dalloway* only pretends to be inventive and "continues until the end to pretend to be, what it is not."

She sometimes couldn't read the papers. But Woolf always began a new project as soon as she finished the last, and her dedication to work itself tells us something about what a successful life can look like. Highs breaking through months of gray; driven by persistence.

Woolf's product from novel to novel was almost embarrassingly uneven. I think she wrote many of the worst, along with many of the best, lines in history. Sometimes reading a line in Woolf I want to jump from my chair— giddy that *she's not so good*! It's lovely. She's human. But she valued the ongoing work for the work itself, and her life shows what a steady dedication to a goal can amount to. She rarely had a sense of when she was good but trusted in the payoff of a consistent output.

Early experiences helped seal her idea about "success." As said, she had what would today be most likely diagnosed as bipolar disorder, and one of her most pronounced depressions happened when she was twenty-two, when her father died, and she suffered auditory hallucinations where birds sang in Greek, she couldn't sleep, and she attempted suicide by jumping out of a window. During part of this illness, Virginia moved in with a family friend I mentioned earlier, Violet Dickinson. This convalescence was a respite with another woman she trusted, and in the meaningful recovery period Violet gave Virginia some strategies she'd keep with her from then on: You're not going to find stability in other people, Violet showed her. Your parents and siblings are dying; one (Laura, who lived in an asylum) has gone crazy; love is also a violently changing thing. What you need to be happy is to find useful work.

Before that visit, Virginia's emotions had half-hitched to writing, but were still searching for targets. She was passionate with several women in her life, and most likely had a crush on Violet. But Violet helped shift her interests: There would be no love affair here. Instead, she flamed Virginia's sense of ambition, and got her her first publishing gig. Through Violet's connections, Virginia published her first piece of journalism in *The Guardian* in December 1904. Then Violet told her to write—she told the girl to pursue the one thing that wouldn't leave her. She essentially gave her a wonderful lesson: People change but work is constant. A happy person is a person who has steady creative work.

· · · · ·

"HAPPINESS—WHAT I WONDER constitutes happiness?" Woolf wrote in her diary in 1919. "I daresay the most important element is work." When she got healthy, she did turn increasingly to work as a stabilizing principle. Life with her husband encouraged a cycling of creative activities. After writing in the morning, she turned to those other hobbies that diverted her mind, like the long walks and setting type for the Hogarth Press, the printer they'd set up in their basement. Work on "the Press . . . prevents brooding; & gives me something solid to fall back on," she wrote in her diary on August 2, 1924. That is: Find central work, then find backup work. Do something creative, and bolster it with diversions that feed the ego.

·····

WOOLF'S SECRET TO KEEPING moodiness at bay: Find activity that you have some control in. She needed work to exercise her personality. Daily work that gives you no sense of creative freedom won't cut it. We need some constant outlet that challenges you, she said. A challenge isn't hard to find: some activity in which you're making decisions that influence the outcome of this work. Some work that bends to your imagination. Some work that shows you new sides of yourself.

·····

THE SAME IDEAS WERE echoed in a therapy group I moderate for recovering alcoholics. One group member became a marathoner after quitting drinking, and recently told the group there's a difference between the pleasures you get from running and from drinking. The more you put into your running habit, he said, the more you get out; and it's the reverse with drinking, which gives you less the more you give it. His definition of rewarding exertion was one Woolf would agree with: You've got to find a hobby that grows, rather than shrinks, as you feed it.

The writing goals Woolf set for herself were particularly difficult. In those marathoner's terms, she had to feed this hobby *a lot*. Woolf basically wanted to invent a literary style that accurately portrayed the mind as it moves through memories, moods, and desires. She thought traditional literature was all too clean, with its dominant tragic and epic plots. "Things don't happen in one's mind like that," she wrote in her diary on February 12, 1927. She wanted to craft a new type of book that would drop its fast-forward motion to capture what feels so much messier as we actually live, moment to moment. She wanted to write in a style that conveyed our internal experience while still holding together as a well-directed plot.

· · · · ·

SHE TRIED EVERYTHING. FROM a young age, she kept diaries. She let herself ramble, even sometimes in her journalism, which she wrote a lot of.

Depicting emotion was hard; creating a new genre was hard. Being original was often embarrassing, because the work tended to be uneven. Looking back over her own pages, Woolf was often hurt by her own inconsistency. The writing was sometimes brilliant, but those spots were flanked with sloppy or boring parts. Accepting her process meant admitting her imperfections. She found peace through a simple idea: Smart things *will be uneven.* "I'm not going to be popular," she writes in her diary in February 1922, "So . . . I'm to write what I like; & they're to say what they like. My only interest as a writer lies, I begin to see, in some queer individuality. . . . But then I say to myself, is not 'some queer individuality' precisely the quality I respect?" She would rather express what was distinctly Virginia than try for something polished but less original. In *A Room of One's Own*, Woolf wrote that good novels are always going to be flawed here and there: "Novels do come to grief somewhere. The imagination falters under the enormous strain." Extended expression strains to contain all it sees. But what holds a soulful project together, she wrote, "is something that one calls integrity . . . the conviction . . . that this is the truth." That means running after your distinct possibilities, tugging inconsistency with you.

· · · · ·

IF DOING SOMETHING NEW means being uneven—nailing some gems but also some losers—she had to be as generous as possible with her own inconsistency. Another moment from the alcoholics' therapy group: One woman described her tendency to relapse as a dread of steady work. "I don't want to 'recover' and work," she said. "Work shows me my failures." She'd rather drink and sometimes feel untouchable than be as critical as she sometimes was when she was sober. She highlighted a truth about growth: We deal with our limits in it. Woolf found that we only build self-esteem through accepting who we are.

For Virginia, this self-knowledge meant reading over her early novels and seeing an old self that embarrassed her. She felt occassional torment, wishing she could re-write what she'd done. But she also knew that looking back and thinking "it would have been perfect if I had changed [X]" was a dream. The fact is that every change you make on an old project would actually force you to think of a new edit. We don't create smooth things; knowing this means becoming familiar with what is particular about your skills and personality. You create an original product after accepting what makes you distinct.

• • • • •

VIRGINIA SOMETIMES HATED HOW her novels showed her old selves. Her first novel's girlish, anxious, energetic prose made her "cheeks burn," she wrote in her diary on February 4, 1920. But she could admit her young self had guts, too: "How gallantly she takes her fences . . . I can do little to amend," Woolf wrote. She's accepting the form of the personality she has.

On August 2, 1924, Woolf wrote a rule in her diary: "If we didn't live venturously . . . trembling over precipices, we should never be depressed." She's forty-two, accepting the fact that depression is the price she pays for the life she lives: Big minds are often depressed, disappointed, mean, crass, and shortsighted. Tough work brings tension, and it's usually the conflicted minds that take big steps.

• • • • •

HONESTLY EXPERIENCING YOUR OWN highs and failures is awfully uncomfortable. Writing is particularly hard. Joyce, Sartre, and other writers have also recorded this in their letters and diaries. Writing was like a violent trip, in which they learned what they hadn't known about themselves. ("Writing in English is the most ingenious torture ever devised for sins committed in previous lives," James Joyce wrote.) Writing is exposure and exploration. It can also be like sleepwalking in the nude, because you say things but don't know how others, reading in their own beds, see you.

Virginia knew the impossibility of getting a perfect read on her own progress, so she had an ethic of persistence, which said that if she followed her own instinct long enough, she'd produce something of value. She didn't control or know how each word would sound, so simply trusted in the process. You move forward as if in a cloud, faithful that a life of earnest work will pay you back.

A Study

Since Virginia's death, a psychologist, Dean Simonton, has published a theory that explains the importance of this idea—of working on without full insight about your progress at each point. In his "equal-odds" rule, for which he studied the career of thousands of creative minds, from poets to composers to mathematicians, he shows that people produce their masterpieces when they're most productive.

That is: You keep a surprisingly consistent ratio of better to less-successful work. You're the same you, creating the *sort of stuff you make*. In the years when you do the most, you'll create both your biggest mass of great works and your highest number of failures. Simonton goes on to call the artistic process a surrender to who we are, even when we don't understand the inner machine: Our creativity "is to some significant degree blind or haphazard. This [essentially] means . . . the individual has no a priori way of foreseeing which . . . combinations will prove most fruitful." The best you can do is to keep working—and to trust in statistics: As you produce more, you increase your chances of success.

The science basically shows we've got to work consistently—without trying to figure out how well we're doing at each little step. Just trust that when you do more, you have a better shot at spitting out your "masterpiece."

• • • • •

IN THAT SPIRIT OF unrelenting forward motion, Woolf wrote for about three to eight hours a day, and the result is that she finally did produce the books she's known for. What Simonton called steady production helped her get identity onto the page.

Two weeks before she turned thirty-eight, she was still

struggling at her desk, moving her pen around and figuring out how to express the mind without losing her plotline. She was recovering from a sickness, unsure of herself, but now felt a sort of rush. The pen scribbled. She wrote a short story, "An Unwritten Novel," which was about ten pages that seemed to accomplish what she wanted.

She worked on it near her birthday, too. She recorded joy in her diary, January 26, 1920: "The day after my birthday; in fact I'm 38. . . . This afternoon [I] arrived at some idea of a new form for a new novel. . . . What the unity shall be I have yet to discover: the theme is a blank to me; but I see immense possibilities."

Six months later, she published the short story in the magazine *London Mercury*, and then she struggled on, not yet bringing the vision to a bigger fruition. At forty she published the novel *Jacob's Room* (critics almost universally call her first two novels before *Jacob's Room* "conventional" in comparison), which was one step closer. She went on to play and search and fail and cry and work until August 1923, at the age of forty-one. Then she turned to her diary one evening and burst with discovery: "I should say a good deal about *The Hours* [her manuscript, which became *Mrs. Dalloway*] & my discovery; how I dig out beautiful caves behind my characters." Two months later: I "discover[ed] what I call my tunneling process. . . . This is my prime discovery so far; & the fact that I've been so long finding it, proves, I think . . . that you can [not] do this sort of thing consciously. One feels about in a state of misery—indeed I made up my mind one night to abandon the book [*Mrs. Dalloway*, which she was working on]—& then one touches the hidden spring."

These weren't just euphoric scribblings—Woolf really did, at forty-one, deliver the breakthrough that came with constant high output. She solved a lifelong problem about literary form, inventing a new style. She was able to combine thought and action in her fiction by focusing on characters' memories. In her "tunneling" technique, as she called it, Woolf would sit in a character's perspective until his recollection ran up against his daily activity. Her *Mrs. Dalloway* and *To the Lighthouse*, which followed, are novels that both re-create the mind and rush forward with a plot better than any of her other work. They are, as Simonton and the psychologists labeled this sort of thing above, her masterpieces.

· · · · ·

So that was joy—many consecutive years of writing nearly every day paid off. But it's also important to remember that the success never felt perfect, and after she'd had her breakthrough, she wrote other sloppy, irrelevant books. She didn't reach some plane that ensured further success. From the beginning, success was something she'd hit in bits, and miss more than she hit. The philosophy was this: If you put away a segment of regular time for your projects, and continue through the inconsistencies, and simply keep at it, you're going to realize your potential better than if you don't attack the work.

· · · · ·

WOOLF'S ETHIC ABOUT SHAMELESSLY keeping a schedule is the sort of strategy that works with mundane things, too. You can't get in shape by going to the gym with gusto every now and again. The only strategy that really works is committing yourself to a productive routine. It's like closing your eyes to what's happening in the moment, trusting consistency itself. You don't see your body change from day to day. You accept the idea of long-term work—if I keep at it, Virginia knew, then something's got to come of this.

The ethic of a schedule also means finding balance when you fall off the beam. Accept a superficial example: All dieting books tell you to ignore the scattered failings. If you eat too much cake one afternoon, don't try to radically make up for it the next day by fasting. Instead, accept that you sometimes mess up, but that the whole point of routine is the larger-scale statistics of it. Don't let one day's crisis unravel the overall pattern. Instead of correcting yourself with a fast, enjoy the slip. Then forget it and go back to the diet. Said again: Failures are part of the normal statistical arch and don't affect the larger picture much.

Going steady-ahead means accepting that you can't see yourself from above—that you are always *you*, and not necessarily the perfect judge of every moment. Dedication to work means just moving on, with respect for larger statistics and the goal.

• • • • •

WOOLF'S DAILY WORK DIDN'T need to be phenomenal. When working on *Mrs. Dalloway*, she wrote fifty to two hundred words a day. This paragraph here is fifty words, and although producing anything isn't easy, it isn't impossible either. Woolf woke each day to write the images and scenes she could.

• • • • •

THE PERSISTENCE CAN MEAN success. The difference between a breakthrough and an uneventful life might just be the difference between a lower and a higher threshold for actual—painful, self-exposing—work.

CHAPTER 7

Lie to Encourage Your Friends

THAT ALL SOUNDS FINE—work every day and you'll achieve something. But Virginia also knew something else. No matter how much you feel at peace with your work, you won't be satisfied without also getting some positive feedback. That is, we can happily claim that we do what we do for *ourselves alone*, but we'd also starve without other people's input. For example, painting is a hobby I've had for a while. I'm not very good. But I'm not awful either. I verge on the edge. One day I was painting in my room, unsure about whether to finish this picture. My relationship to it rose up and down according to whatever voice, supportive or judgmental, I heard in my head.

At one point, my cousin walked in and said, "That's *fantastic!*" His words, which were just a casual comment in his world, were enough to shift the very colors in my mind—the way the whole wall looked. This was a phenomenon that Virginia understood: Your evaluation of something varies with other people's responses. You don't want it to, but it does. You can have a wonderful sense of self, and produce good work, but you simply won't be happy about it without feeling that other people get it.

This fact implies at least one interpersonal clue: If you've got a friend who's working hard on some project, and she comes to you with some half-baked thing, holding it up with anticipation—and you don't like the project but trust her energy—you might lie about your opinion. Short of lying, you can work hard to emphasize the bright spots. I can respect my friend's ability to do future work, which means relaxing my own need to judge or feel correct.

Virginia had smart things to say about the generosity we crave and can give to each other in her essay "How Should One Read a Book?" In it she describes the feeling of judgment as it happens. She says when we're unsure, we sometimes make ourselves into harsh or unforgiving crit-ics. Perhaps we feel pressure to have smart, final verdicts on creative projects because the world's judge, History, shows no empathy when he passes through. It's as if we want to match an ideal image of smarts, so we stiffen when asked to assess something an amateur creates.

But Woolf reminds us that we often move too quickly in judging others. We tend to buy into our opinions, to pass a more concrete judgment than we're justified to do. She offers a new suggestion for how to engage with our friends: by launching a *discussion* of the work—looking at themes, expanding ideas—rather than baldly assessing that the work's a "success" or "failure." "If by our means"—if through ranging, thoughtful input—"books were to be-come stronger, richer, and more varied," she writes in her essay, "that would be an end worth reaching."

• • • • •

To SEE HOW WOOLF encountered generosity in her own working life, sink into what might be the most poi-gnant time in her writing career. She was fifty-four, work-ing on her eighth novel, *The Years*. She had had good success by this point in her life but still felt nagged by critics. She'd written her masterpieces, *Mrs. Dalloway, To the Light-house*, and *The Waves*, as well as published *A Room of One's Own*, a groundbreaking piece of feminist nonfiction. But she felt the return of self-doubt—remembering critics like Arnold Bennett and Wyndham Lewis who accused her of being a bourgeois, irrelevant writer. In response, she wanted to write a book in a new voice, using more concrete descriptions than usual. Seeing fascism emerge in Spain and Germany, she also wanted to make this novel more overtly political, to give a more direct description of war and class.

For five years, through her early fifties, she searched for a new appropriate voice. She scrawled nine hundred pages and cut them back to four hundred. She first envisioned this book as a mix of essays and fiction, but then rethought it as a traditional novel.

She spent such a tedious five years on it that her income lagged. For one of the first times in their marriage, Leonard told her that she hadn't earned enough to pay her share of the living expenses.

Then, when she finished her draft, she feared it was a failure. Wanting to protect herself—and though she always showed Leonard her writing before sending it out—she mailed the manuscript to her printer without Leonard's seeing it. When the printer's proofs came back for her last edit, she got sick looking at them. She hated this book.

· · · · ·

IN THE MONTHS THAT followed, Woolf hit her worst depression in twenty-two years, with insomnia, eating problems, and headaches. Leonard begged her to stop her work editing the proofs, and they took a break, driving around the country. Virginia spent a shaky summer doing limited editing on the printer's proofs in their summer house.

At the end of 1936, trying to finish her edit, she ran up against a seeming dead end. Around noon on November 2, she brought everything to Leonard and told him to burn the book. She went for a walk through London, wanting calm. Maybe, she thought, she'd been lying to herself too long. She had no talent and should face the music. That surrender felt nice, in a way, as she wrote in her diary: "Now I was no longer Virginia, the genius, but only a perfectly insignificant yet content—shall I call it spirit? a body? And very tired. Very old."

Once home from an hour's walk, she told Leonard she'd just make money through journalism (which she'd always considered a lesser art). She'd write more book reviews for *The Times*. Over the next few hours, she experienced an ongoing roller coaster. Friends came over, and they found distraction by going to a book show in town. Home again, Virginia sank, and Leonard tried to cheer her up by reading her manuscript. Maybe it wasn't so bad, he said. She did loosen up a little watching him. In her diary, she wrote she felt her mind rise with possibility as he read—maybe he'd offer a new perspective; and if so, she could pull a full reversal. She could feel in control again.

He read through the evening, while she paced and slept. He turned to her late at night, and managed, with the manuscript collapsed in his lap, to say it was working: "Extraordinarily good," he said, "as good as any of them," as she wrote in her diary on November 3. He read on. On November 4, at midnight, he finished reading this long book of hers, *The Years*. He looked up at her, with tears in his eyes.

· · · · ·

COLLAPSE THE SCENE TO his head before we hear what he said. Leonard later wrote an autobiography that gave this confession: He thought this long book was about the worst thing she'd written. It was "inordinately long and loose," he wrote, "slightly dead even at the moment of birth." But "I knew that unless I could give a completely favourable verdict she would be in despair and would have a very serious breakdown. . . . The verdict on *The Years* which I now gave her was not absolutely and completely what I thought about it." He knew she was smart. This work wasn't her best. But he looked up and gave her the fuel she needed. It was "a most remarkable book," he said, words she echoed in her diary on November 5.

• • • • •

THE WORD WAS ENOUGH to light a complete upswing for Virginia. The "relief was divine," she wrote. "So amazing is the reversal since Tuesday morning." She went back to the novel, shortened it because he suggested she might, and sent it back to be printed. The events that followed surprised both of them.

Virginia Woolf had been relatively successful up to this point, age fifty-four. She had made just enough money at forty-five, with her novel *To the Lighthouse*, to buy a car. She'd made a little more with *Orlando*. But when this eigth novel, *The Years*, came out, luck aligned. People had heard enough about Woolf by now to want to buy her latest book. It was also an easier read than the earlier ones. When the publisher released it in America, *The Years* became her first bestseller there. It stayed on the bestsellers list in America for weeks, and within one year, Virginia's book earnings increased by five and a half times, from 634 pounds in 1936 to 3,426 pounds in 1937.

• • • • •

BUT LET'S REVISIT LEONARD in the hot seat. The man was able to save his wife's artistic life by telling her a generous lie, and we should think about how and why he did it. Leonard was as serious about writing as she was. He was a political thinker, writing books of his own (forty-three pamphlets and books to Virginia's twenty-five) and editing five major magazines during his lifetime. Both he and Virginia were attuned to the artist's struggle, and they printed their friends' avant-garde work from their basement. They loved the risks of creativity and valued encouraging expression more than baldly judging it.

Leonard also knew, as Virginia suggests in her essay on reading, that we tend to experience overblown pride when we're asked to judge. Leonard did everything he could to take a more generous approach to her work. He knew his judgment of this book that nearly killed his wife was skewed. He didn't flatly enjoy reading what she'd wrangled with, but strangers would engage with the book differently than he did. Even in those moments when his opinions felt like the only ones, he had to remember they weren't. "What laws can be laid down about books?" Virginia writes in her own essay. "Is Hamlet a better play than Lear?"— and who should be the final judge? "Nobody," she writes. "To admit authorities [to] tell us how to read [or] what value to place upon what we read, is to destroy the spirit of freedom which is the breath of [art]."

· · · · ·

LEONARD ALSO KNEW A fact about experience: An artist lives through a different trip than her audience does. Someone who makes art foresees a future that others don't yet see. Imagine someone who's midway through a sentence at some party. He's drinking; he's high; he flings a hand across the room and launches an idea. You come in mid-sentence and—hearing only half his idea—think he might be too in love with himself, too naïve. You might want to edit his sentence, to set it right. But in her essay Virginia urges us to remember a difference in spirit: The judge doesn't experience the same energy that the artist does. The judge or outsider hears half a sentence; he's tired; he likes his own voice more than this drunker stranger's; and the performance sounds unfinished. But to the performer and whomever he's carrying, "It may be one letter—but what a vision it gives!" Woolf writes in this essay. "It may be a few sentences—but what vistas they suggest!" Art comes with a forward momentum—and the tired, excluded, or outsider judge is often premature if he silences what he simply doesn't get yet. It's important to remember the different perspectives inside and outside the active mind, and let a visionary move forward if we know our attack is powered by a need to look equally creative or smart.

• • • • •

YOUR JUDGMENT OF A friend's idea or project actually never needs to be as stiff as a "yes" or "no." A *conversation* about the work is better, Woolf writes. Avoid being the critic who thinks he's in a "shooting gallery," she writes in her essay, with "only one second in which to load and aim and shoot." The machismo's probably just self-protection.

Leonard might have embellished his praise of *The Years* simply to be sweet to his wife, but what he said was also partly true. Almost anything someone spends five years on will have the stamp of effort, and will be interesting, if rough. That's a simple nice fact about hard effort: It does put grain or tooth into something. There are probably two types of art or production: the stuff that slips out fast in a rush, as Woolf said some of her novels, like *To the Lighthouse*, did; and the stuff, like *The Years*, which almost kills you. The fast work is almost always the cleaner and better work. But the work that takes long, if less smooth, has its own value. It shows the working hand. It just shows another— and very real—part of who we are. It expresses the side of you that is not clean but is engaged in something new. *The*

Years is that tougher type of book—not as fluid a read as *To the Lighthouse*, but a good novel to dive into during a long, investigative summer.

• • • • •

THIS IS SOMETHING LIKE what Picasso knew when he let a friend, Clouzot, film him at work on paintings to show how, through layers of revision, he recast his image dozens of times, thinking his way through it. Certainly Picasso was also an artist who knew how to whiz off a painting in a second—slapping three brush strokes on a dinner plate. But in the movie *The Mystery of Picasso*, Picasso honored the edit, painting image after revising image after revising image, until the final product was nothing like its sketch in the beginning.

Another story: In writing *Madame Bovary*, Flaubert fought a well-known struggle of tears and self-hatred. "I brood more over an ill-suited word than I rejoice over a well-proportioned paragraph," he wrote to a friend. In almost half a year, he reported, he wrote only sixty pages, working continuously, but throwing out far more than he kept. His young niece grew up around such a ridiculous self-battery called struggle, she actually assumed the word "Bovary" meant "work."

And So

In the spirit of their relationship (the ideas she put in writing and he also practiced), Leonard was able to read Virginia's work, see imperfection, and still lie to her. He told her the work was "remarkable." It gave her the fuel she needed to finish and publish the thing. Leonard was able to admit he wasn't the final judge on all production—that other people read differently than he did. He relaxed his need to *judge* and he encouraged the creative instinct. The decision was a gift to both of them. Woolf got her first American bestseller, and with it energy for five more years of fiction writing.

CHAPTER 8

Find a Political Voice

IT'S TIME TO HIT Virginia's famous weakness. Although she wrote passionately about social issues, her critics have often called her an abstract dreamer, and so a weak political mind. Virginia sometimes felt the same about herself—that she couldn't find the voice to practically influence the issues she cared about. Although she wrote two aggressive nonfiction political books, *A Room of One's Own* and *Three Guineas*, she thought women often went unheard in political circles.

Woolf was a pacifist—and enjoyed the company of her friends with that idea through World War I. But as Hitler rose to power during the last stage of her life, most of Virginia's contemporaries changed their stance. Seeing a need to fight against fascism, her husband gave lectures and wrote articles arguing for rearmament.

Woolf never endorsed war during her life; her unflagging political interest was gender. She argued that because men have held power so long, we've come to value competition more than we might otherwise have. In *Three Guineas* she argues there's no fundamental difference between the Nazis and other embodiments of masculine power: Western society is built on a foundation of ego and dominance. We're living a silly sexual role-play, she said: Men parade their knowledge to win a good education, high-paying jobs, and political debates. Women silently support that rat race by giving them the attention they ask for. Woolf said we could radically rethink our thirst for dominance. Because women never did have an equal stake in Western society, they might as well name themselves an "Outsiders' Society." This society, Woolf writes in *Three Guineas*, would break the cycle of power by treating men with "an attitude of complete indifference."

She offers a useful analogy: Imagine there's a boy who keeps tooting his annoying toy horn in your yard. If you want him to stop, you need the right strategy. It would be ineffective to directly *tell* him to stop. He'd actually enjoy the attention and go back to his horn whenever he wanted some more. Instead, Woolf writes, you've got to ignore the horn altogether, so that the game no longer pays him back. Then he eventually has to find another way to connect with the world.

· · · · ·

WOOLF'S MAIN CONTRIBUTION TO modern politics was probably the idea that the personal is the political (not her language), which became the rallying call behind the second wave of American feminism in the 1960s and '70s. Woolf said that the way we interact in our relationships reflects a society's larger dynamics. We have to remodel conversation on the small scale to redirect a country's larger ethics.

· · · · ·

BUT WITH HER STRONG political ideas, Woolf was also caught in a bind. Her hatred for those speeches performed at podiums partly entailed a surrender of her own distinct political voice. Woolf asked us to ignore the "horn" altogether, and she felt more comfortable in the world of poetic language—choosing fiction over cloying public dogma. But as Hitler gathered power, Woolf felt increasingly ineffective in her silence. As her husband spoke up against the Nazis, Woolf thought even he was misguided. He gave speeches in which he, too, was "hawking his conscience," arrogant like a "tub thumper," she wrote in her diaries. In a September 11, 1940, letter to Ethel, Woolf said that even her own beloved fiction seemed increasingly irrelevant. "It's odd to feel one's writing in a vacuum—no-one will read it. I feel the audience has gone."

Virginia and Leonard had hoarded pills to kill themselves if Hitler invaded London. Through the winter of 1940, they listened as the bombs came in, and their London house was destroyed. On March 28, 1941, Woolf's depression grew, and she hallucinated voices, which she hadn't done in years. In a last act of self-silencing, she drowned herself in the River Ouse. Of course she didn't only kill herself because of war, but her final depression gives insight into how this woman approached practical life, and how we might learn from her struggle in shaping our own political voices.

A psychologist helps explain how Woolf went from a sense of frustration to a sense of defeat. In his 1960s studies of depression, Martin Seligman defined the phenomenon of "learned helplessness." In his study he submitted dogs to a series of shocks. After suffering these shocks with no means of escape, the dogs bought into the idea that they had no influence on their world. When Seligman put the dogs into cages that freely allowed for escape and shocked them again, they just lay down and took the punishment. Seligman called the shift "learned helplessness": They had assumed a long-standing, pervasive sense of impotence. Seligman extended the idea to human depression: When we shift from a rather healthy skepticism that says, "My influence is limited," to a more totalizing and static claim that "I have *no influence*," we distort our stance in the world. Seligman said that the key to self-esteem is keeping nuance in your claims about yourself—which is a struggle you've probably experienced. There are days in which we're able to speak with balance ("I have *some* power to change things") and days in which energy collapses to a fixed exaggeration ("I ruin everything I touch"). Seligman argues that happiness depends on moderating your idea of how capable you are.

Woolf swung to an exaggeration of defeat in her political writing. Although she is the master of nuance in her fiction—in which no character lives in *utter* isolation or *endless* depression but is constantly buoyed by a harmonizing impulse—in her politics Woolf introduces a starker black and white. *Three Guineas* stages enemies and victims, right and wrong. Here men have power; women have no voice. Men make war; women would make peace. She doesn't promote compromise as much as a totalizing shutdown, a collapse. Men and women, Woolf warns, speak across a chasm: "It seems plain that we think differently according as we are born differently; there is [your] point of view [and my] point of view. All differ." Looking across the dinner table at a man, she feels "a gulf so deeply cut between us that [I wonder] whether it is any use to try to speak across it." She writes that culture has sent the genders down different roads. Men have enjoyed power so long—and women have so long played the silent helpmate—that we can hardly speak honestly to each other anymore.

Although it's impossible to know what another person's depression feels like, some things are clear in this case. When Seligman observed the dogs who would not rile themselves to escape, he said they had assumed an exaggerated self-concept: They lived as if none of their behaviors had real-world effects, and so missed the chance to escape a shock when they could. Although Woolf often knew her own influence on the world (*Three Guineas* is, after all, a book addressed to a fictional man, as if dialogue *works*), she strikes the pose of surrender, too—as that outsider whose voice is nothing but an unheard whisper to the men around her. That stance is one that Seligman calls fatal—one that needs its balance in what an earnest mind *does* achieve.

Woolf's struggle looks poignant from our position. When—in the literature classes I teach—we get to the section of *Three Guineas* in which Woolf calls for her Outsiders'

Society, some of my students always laugh: "She's hardly an *outsider*," they say. "She was *part of* the tradition. She quotes white men like Shakespeare and Tennyson all the time." And from this perspective in time, that observation looks right. We do see a woman who was in rich conversation with the world around her. The point is that Woolf sometimes felt that defeat that could drive a "suppressed [female] poet [to] dash . . . her brains out on the moor [and] about the highways crazed with the torture that her gift had put her to." She didn't always see how—with each of her books—she was gradually remodeling the ways in which we think of power, gender, and identity.

Revolution

One way of thinking about an individual's influence is remembering that our perspectives are distorted when we're doing things. While we're active in change, we don't see our movements from above—so don't fully know what we're doing as we go. We act in steps; and if we are moving forward, people in the future see a larger, more definitive sweep. Consider how history moved through most revolutions—in progressive steps that the players involved didn't fully appreciate at the time. We went from hamlets to the cities of the Industrial Revolution through smaller advances in mining, canals, trains, and spinning jennies; and no single moment contained the perspective that history gives. We also went from segregation to a postapartheid South Africa through stages, from underground resistance to strikes—to international sanctions, cultural movements, and the actions of a few great leaders. Significant moments built upon each other without the picture of the final result. Lech Walesa was a shipyard worker who could not see the scope of his influence from any one point in his journey. He was stuck in jail in 1981, just eight years before he'd become the first postcommunist president in Poland. After his release, he was still subject to government restriction off and on for the next eight years. During this time, he often reported that the effort felt useless. But tenacity brought changes: With reviving force, Walesa was soon elected Poland's new democratic leader.

Think of an ant-on-the-bridge analogy—or what it feels like to walk over a bridge with a big arc. From a distance, the walk looks exhausting. But being close to the ground distorts perspective, so that when you're at the base, the land seems to flatten out. You start to walk without feeling as if you're on the tough lift in the bridge yet. You wait for that impossible rise, but soon enough you're on the other side. Proximity to the project flattens it out—which is an effect that influences most human activity. As we move, we can't see ourselves as a distant onlooker does. If Virginia felt helpless when facing the masculine order, she didn't see how much she was accomplishing with each book she wrote. From our spot in history, we see. It's as if history should have the power to cast down a positive word: "You do have influence. Trust me."

Modern Politics

Take that idea to how we all face politics today. Massive change feels impossible, even more so for us than it did for Virginia. The government-corporate behemoth, which today consolidates power in a more solid way than ever, can make any individual feel voiceless. If I want to change Halliburton's policy, I'll certainly intermittently feel *I have no influence.* But the point is that as soon as I buy into the exaggerated idea that "I have no voice at all," then—as Seligman says—you stop using the recourses you do have. As long as you can maintain the idea that "I have a limited voice, but it's still a voice," you remain active enough to do what's possible. Then you begin one of those incremental historical changes—like the movement that built cities or democratic societies. And Woolf was—through dedicated work—often fantastically able to keep her power alight.

A Story

A bright story from Woolf's life: When she was twenty-eight, she was already building her ideas about gender and her exclusion from the male-dominated world around her. She already saw a divide between her lyrical world and politics; she spent all day writing *Melymbrosia*, her first attempt at a novel that ranged from marriage to homosexuality to colonialism to love.

This was also a time when the British navy was nearly the strongest power in the world—at 1910, just before World War I. Virginia felt a far cry from the world of the Queen, of Prime Minister Herbert Henry Asquith or Home Secretary Winston Churchill. But one day, Virginia's friend Horace Cole tugged her away from her writing desk. He had a plan. He wanted to write a letter to the navy, pretending to be an Abyssinian dignitary. They'd request a royal welcome onto the flagship HMS *Dreadnought*.

Virginia, Cole, and four other friends could still *play*—or revel in that sense of potency that comes before you ever think *I can't*. They dressed up, painted their skin dark, put on robes. At Paddington Station, Cole demanded a VIP train from the stationmaster, and they filed into the plush train car. When they arrived at the boat docks, they were saluted with a song and flag and welcomed onto the fleet. The kids spoke in a broken Latin that no one understood, and performed fake ceremonies. At one point, Virginia's friend sneezed so hard, his fake mustache flew off, and he stuck it back on before anyone noticed. They refused to eat onboard unless the boat staff wore white gloves. When it was all over, they laughed the whole way back to London. They sent a letter and photo to the newspaper the *Daily Mirror*, telling the British public about their act.

· · · · ·

IT'S INTERESTING TO TRY to remember our potency by thinking of scenes like this, which seem to pop right out of mundane life with possibility. Was there ever a time in which you bridged the gap, touching something you thought impossible to touch? That's the spirit in which we *keep on*, in which we think big change is still possible. At her strongest, Virginia retained a sense of play and fantastic possibility. And at her strongest, she reminds us to do the same with ourselves.

CHAPTER 9

Be Aware of Prejudice

WOOLF EXTENDED HER POLITICAL question in her antiwar book, *Three Guineas*, to try to figure out how prejudice works. In one place in the book, she takes out *Whitaker's Almanack* and looks up government salaries, finding that men make a lot more than women do, and trying to figure out why. She lists the obvious reasons: More men graduate from Oxford and Cambridge, so get good jobs; because of family obligations, women often defer their careers; and because men have been able to sit for college entrance and civil service exams for longer than women have, they score better. She also suggests that men are reluctant to hire women because of dominant stereotypes: Women are less reliable. They're thought to gossip; they get sick.

Then Woolf thinks longer about the real way prejudice works. She says that even though we can review the problems in our institutions, and set out strategies for correcting them, this highly *conscious* work still fails to target some of the ways we actually discriminate. Conscious work can revamp certain laws and procedures, but social tendencies might outlast the change in protocol. For instance, we can write laws to get women on the boards of agencies and divisions of businesses, but the people on those boards are always susceptible to bias:

> . . . a board is not made literally of oak, nor a division of iron.
>
> Both boards and divisions transmit human sympathies, and reflect human antipathies . . . the ties of blood and friendship are recognized. Thus it is quite possible that the name "Miss" transmits through the board or division some vibration which is not registered in the examination room. "Miss" transmits sex; and sex may carry with it an aroma. "Miss" may carry with it the swish of petticoats, the savour of scent or other odour percep-

tible to the nose on the further side of the partition and obnoxious to it.

She wants us to think about the contexts in which we hear words, which she also later defines as "atmosphere." Atmosphere is the feeling a word connotes, and "a very mighty power," she writes in *Three Guineas*. "An epic poem might be written about atmosphere, or a novel in ten or fifteen volumes."

Here's a case of atmosphere: I'm supposed to help hire someone for the dean's office. First a young white man comes in, and I think he's a little arrogant but pretty smart. We shake hands and say good-bye. The next candidate who comes in is black. Even with a conscious resistance to prejudice, I *see* his race. I simply feel the weight of how people have interacted through history. I might pull out a chair for him with more overt courtesy than normal. I might nod more than usual. I might perform a happy acceptance. Even these subtle shifts in my behavior *affect* our interaction— they foreground that *something strange has happened.* That strange thing is Race.

That's what Woolf called the "scent" of a word; in her text she focused on "Miss," writing that words carry connotations that run deeper than our conscious control.

They're weighted by a tremendous social history. You can insist that you see no difference between "Miss" and "Mrs.," but the words still carry an influential "scent," as Woolf described it. They've been used to categorize women according to their married lives, and so carry the trace of sex. It's not easy to shed the feeling of history by making a simple, conscious decision to see things clearly.

In fact, recent studies have shown that it's impossible to shed the residue around a politically loaded word or situation that's long-designated a prejudicial line through race or sex. Woolf didn't live to see the 1990s discovery of what Claude Steele—a black liberal thinker at Stanford who has publicly butted heads with his twin brother, conservative think tank power and *Harper's* editor Shelby Steele—has named Stereotype Threat. Stereotype Threat is an effect in which we unconsciously and unwittingly conform to stereotypes—largely because we're struggling to avoid them. Steele and his colleague Joshua Aronson ran a test in which they gave black and white students a difficult test like the SAT, telling half the group that the test measured intellectual ability, and telling the other half it was simply a set of questions. The half that imagined that they were in an SAT-type scenario conformed to the stereotypical gap between white and black scores, with blacks underscoring. In the other group, the discrepancy didn't happen. In other words, the stereotype about how people score in ability tests like the SAT actually affects how we answer questions in front of us. This effect is largely unconscious. We might consciously disagree with a social myth but still reveal its effects. We spend so much energy resisting the negative role we're expected to play that we underscore exactly when we're expected to.

The same "stereotype threat" has been tested in other areas, from race to gender, age, and weight. People only need to be subtly reminded of their roles in a group to conform to its public persona. In one study by Michael Inzlicht and Talia Ben-Zeev, women in a room with men performed worse on math tests than women in a room without men. They even performed increasingly worse as the number of men in the room increased. Those usually at the higher end of scores suffered from the effect the worst, probably because they struggled to avoid it more. The idea is that what Woolf called "atmosphere" is an unspoken force—the gravitational force around a public idea.

· · · · ·

WHAT WE SEE HERE is that forces take hold in the public realm that aren't easily redirected with a conscious decision to *live fairly*. Woolf suggested that we can't claim equality through a bold assertion that we know what fairness is and are making laws that will fully circumscribe it. She's basically urging the same humility she urges when it comes to personal relationships—crediting the unconscious as playing a role. You can't come into a situation and claim you see and know the forces in action. You can't claim full power to redirect current forces. We can and should work to reshape the public realm by setting new laws and protocols. But at no point should we be so proud of our work that we claim we've accounted for the full terrain. Woolf wants to shine her light on "atmosphere"—those forces like Stereotype Threat that act without our always knowing, and certainly without our ability to immediately redirect them.

· · · · ·

To see another example of "atmosphere," think of the way Joe Louis made his way into the boxing ring. The rules were supposedly fair. George Dixon was the first black world champion in 1890, and Jack Johnson had since become the first black heavyweight champion. Louis was on relatively even ground as far as the sport's guidelines went. But he reportedly once told a friend who was coming up in the boxing world that the only way to be a successful black fighter was to *always* knock out the other guy. You had to be that much better to simply be allowed to return. A black fighter would be seen through an unacknowledged critical lens. It's as if Louis would move against the backdrop of another silhouette, the stereotypical black man. An audience would check his action against that outline.

The form also pulls him to it like a magnet. He's influenced in unseen ways, largely off the books, in chatter. Newspapers framed Louis in ways they didn't acknowledge they were doing. Before he knocked out the famous Primo Carnera in 1935, the newspapers generally transcribed Louis's interviews in dialect. After his victory, fewer did. There was a shift—though there was residue. The *Washington Post* stuck to its guns in typecasting Louis, quoting his response to a question like this: "ah jes kept hittin 'im." That is, the man was framed in solid but publicly unacknowledged ways by social forces.

Go deeper with this if you want. He had to play with unspoken rules. His manager John Roxborough, who managed the betting circles in Detroit, gave Louis seven guidelines for not offending white Americans, including never being photographed with a white woman, never boasting over your white opponent when he's down, never engaging in fixed fights, and living clean. There were different sets of standards for the races.

Woolf said the same for the sexes—that a disenfranchised group doesn't only deal with its hurdles, but lacks the language to describe those hurdles to the mainstream. That's because a lot of discrimination has no public description; some of the most pervasive lines in society are not recognized in law or even in common language.

· · · · ·

WOOLF WANTED TO UNDERSCORE the parts of our social lives that have no words yet. She wanted to look at the powerful but unnamed strands of the social fabric. She tells a wonderful story about the first time she wanted to argue that "atmosphere" existed. She was in her early twenties, not yet having published a novel or gone to school. She read alone. But her brothers were hosting their Cambridge friends every Thursday for intellectual chats, in which they'd pick some topic to discuss, like "Truth," and debate it. Woolf would watch from the sidelines, occasionally entering in. Entering sometimes felt like rapping on the door of what was already too firmly established. The Cambridge boys had learned theory, together, behind the great white walls of the University. Woolf had a quirkier personal relationship to her books. One day, Hawtrey, a mathematician friend, was arguing some point about books. Woolf wanted to tell him her own take—that such a thing called "atmosphere" existed in the pages of fiction. Hawtrey laughed when she said it, unable to map her strange word against any classical term he'd learned. "Prove it," he said. So she ran off for a novel from her room and spent a while trying to tell him what she meant. Think of the struggle here: Not as dramatic as a black boxer making his way into the ring, this was still important—a woman, Virginia, who had no college education and so none of its lingo, wanted to make her way into the Cambridge boys' debate. She felt the pressure an outsider feels—holding on to an idea that she intuits but which isn't acknowledged in the circle of power. She would have to find new words—and find someone who was patient enough to listen. The Outsider bangs against the door of what's already established, and that's a nameless, difficult task—trying to bring a new concept into the arena that's already so very proud of its definitions.

This effort to introduce the new was essentially Woolf's lifework in fiction and social politics. She was aware of the strong divide between the system already in place and the unacknowledged forces under the radar. She knew an existing system poses as complete, justified, and final. In turn, it ignores unrecognized forces. Woolf did acknowledge that we need to depend on laws themselves to force social change, but she was equally sensitive to the warbling whisper in which we discuss anything new. To counteract the strength of standing laws, she wanted to make us aware of forces that we don't yet acknowledge. This simply means admitting that not all things are conscious yet, and that we need the same self-questioning approach to the social arena as we do to our personal friendships. Rather than shouting about what exists, we need to remember the quieter effects that some people wordlessly feel, in "atmosphere."

CHAPTER 10

Change Routines

VIRGINIA WOOLF WAS A creature of habit. From a young age when she was struggling with mental depression, her doctors encouraged her to keep a tight rein on her activities, advising days tailored with an hour or so of outdoor activity, milk before bed, regular sleep, and not too much work.

The discipline generally worked for her. But she was also an intellectual adventurer, which meant that she would wonder what lay on the other side of routine, and she sometimes got hungry to change up the body's regular cycle. The problem is, it's hard to change a cycle. The side of the self that's comfortable where it already is resists the rerooting. I *could* be rewired but my self-love happens on this current, conscious side of the mind—the self that already enjoys a voice and day-to-day control.

Woolf talked about a fight we wage between habit and potential, and the following five glimpses into her life show the practical ways she dealt with it. She left some clues about how deadening routine can be, and how, with creativity, we might sometimes rattle ourselves out of it.

1.

Are You Cheap?
Spend Money Now and Then

One of Woolf's habits was being cheap. After years of telling herself she was a woman who didn't like buying things, she really played that role, holding back with her money as if by instinct.

She lived with that one idea of "Virginia." Understand what this means: A major part of getting over any personality rut, from drug addiction to stinginess, is remembering that we only *imagine* we're stuck as "this or that" as

Virginia says; in fact, we can radically change. Any lifestyle basically comes from familiarity with certain people and places; change happens when we find new friends and habits to replace the old ones. The problem is that a new life looks amorphous and blank from this side of the divide. But any new rotation *would gain* a more concrete form as it actually got going. Because it's so hard to imagine the actual, different life that can exist, we sometimes need to just take an unmeasured leap, and put a new activity in motion, trusting that we'll feel like an equally solid "me" once that "me" is recast.

So: Woolf was cheap, and had been cheap for years. But one week, after making more money on *Orlando* than she'd ever made on a book before, mild mania ensued and she rode that euphoria for a flash outside her current cycle. On December 17, 1928, she spent money. She recorded it in her diary the next day, writing, "Yesterday I spent 15/- on a steel brooch. I spent £3 on a mother of pearl necklace—& I haven't bought a jewel for 20 years, perhaps! I have carpeted the dining room—& so on. I think one's soul is the better for this lubrication. . . . The important thing is to spend freely, without fuss or anxiety; & to trust to one's power of making more."

That's a great moment in the diary, in which Woolf tries a new behavior and to her surprise feels replenished.

The new routine *works*—and she feels her potential for stepping outside an old convention.

Think of the similarities between cheapness and a strict personal consistency in the first place. Both tendencies lean toward retention. You want to hold on to what you have. You're scared that change will be a letting-go that won't repay you. You fear that risk—of letting go of something you enjoy and getting nothing back from the world.

But here Woolf broke both laws: She spent money and let go of the overdetermined "Virginia." The effect was what she called "soul lubrication"—a feeling that the outside world wasn't as vacant or stingy as she'd feared.

She's talking about letting go of old habits with the faith that a new self can be invented. The scene closely echoes a scene Freud wrote to describe the process of learning about the world's dependability. Freud described his grandson's learning to let go of his mother. For his first year and a half, the grandson worried that his mother would dissolve when she left the room. He worked his way through that anxiety by playing a "fort-da" game, in which he flung a spool of thread, like a yo-yo, away from him and then yanked it back. Playing with his yo-yo like this showed him about constancy, which he needed for independence. You toss what you have away, and see that you get replenished as necessary. Life goes on; the spool comes back. If you can toss out what you own with a sense of calm, say Freud and Woolf, that's strength. If you can relax the fist, a new object will fill it.

The same from the therapist's office: A therapist faces a rigid person and says, "What would happen if you were forced to live in a totally new environment, without the things you now use to make yourself comfortable?"

The answer: The guy would have to rewire himself to new habits and a new description of what "I" is. The fact is that all of us are capable of rewriting ourselves if put in radically new circumstances. The idea of it is daunting before we start, but the whole process gets much easier once we actually start a new activity, make it a routine, and name the emerging personality as "me."

2.

Make Rules for Moods

You're more than one self, and knowing it is useful. Woolf was pushed face-to-face with her own changeability by her bipolar disorder, which made one day's "Virginia" radically different than another's. She was interested in the fact that so many potential selves lived inside, and she knew that mere memory couldn't bridge the divide between them. When you're content, you can't vividly, sensually remember deep depression. So she'd send herself notes across the divide of a mood swing, as if sending notes to a stranger.

· · · · ·

DIARY ON April 10, 1921: "I must note the symptoms of the disease [my depression] so as to know it next time. The first day one's miserable: the second happy."

A couple of days later, on April 12: "I must hurriedly note more symptoms of the disease, so that I can turn back here & medicine myself next time."

These are notes from one Virginia to another.

· · · · ·

THE IDEA IS THAT all of us assume states that vary, from drunkenness to mania to exhaustion. It's important to remember the real difference between these states— and then know we have some options for navigating between them.

For instance, echoing Woolf's strategy for bridging selves, you can make rules to handle gaps in your perspectives:

Never send drunken e-mails to my boss.

Don't make long-term decisions about a relationship when especially tired.

These credos can be freestanding laws that—respecting the real difference between states of mind—take the power away from any one bold but irrational state to wield too much power over the way your life plays out.

I have a friend who discovered he'd always broken off his relationships in the weeks before Valentine's Day. It must have been a subconscious pressure to conform with an ideal love; he'd just break his relationships off. But as soon as he recognized the historical pattern in himself, he simply set himself an indelible rule: Don't break up with people in the two weeks before Valentine's Day. Sensible enough: If it's just the seasonal pressure, he can outlive it by staying true to a freestanding rule. And since he made the rule, the strategy's worked, because one relationship has lasted.

Respecting our alternative moods as truly *different* states of being, we can force ourselves to distinct, physical steps when trying to go from one mood to another. I remember having a hard time shifting from sad to happy one day last summer. I was in Fort Lauderdale, walking down the street, deeply depressed, knowing I had to meet friends for dinner, and killing myself to try to inch into *happy*. It felt impossible to do with mere ideas. The only solution was to go take a jog on the beach. A new movement can so fundamentally shift your perspective and blood flow that a big change can happen.

Woolf wrote about these shifts she'd force herself to take. When feeling dark, she knew she had to put the body, itself, into a new motion. She'd sometimes get on a bus, or wander through strange parts of the city. The sheer physical exhaustion of walking or biking around for an hour (she liked those two most) would change the flow in her bloodstream. "Suppose, I bought a ticket at the museum," she wrote in her diary on March 8, 1941, trying to shake herself out of a rut in her writing. Suppose I "biked in daily and read history. Suppose I selected one dominant figure in every age & wrote round & about." These were strategies for moving the body, on its fast downward slope to depression, into a new activity. She'd give herself assignments to change her course, like this one in the diary on September 8, 1920: "Oh vanity, vanity! how it grows on me—how I swear to crush it out—Learn French is the only thing I can think of." So she'd open up the French grammar book, and get cracking—admitting the reality of our moods, and counteracting them with real activities. In a lab study, psychologists also found that when people listen to happy music, their moods observably, reliably shift. So: Listen to music as a strategy for shifting the head-frame.

· · · · ·

THE IDEA IS THAT you know how different the mind is in its different modes. So you make strategies for moving from one mode to another. You navigate a movement you don't fully control; as you know it's coming, you know what messages to send across the gap.

· · · · ·

ONCE WHEN VIRGINIA WAS facing writer's block, she forced herself to take a long car trip with Leonard. She made herself think of absolutely nothing for the whole trip—play mere tourist for day; eat mindlessly; count road signs—because "I predict that the desire to write will become so frantic by the time we're on the way back that I shall be making up all along the French roads," she wrote in her diary on April 29, 1935. She's essentially saying that while you do have to interrupt your ordinary head with radical new action, you don't have to worry that those shifts are self-erasure. You're not dissolving selves, but rotating the crops, to sweeten production. After the gym or some other forced activity like learning French, your usual head, the dominant and productive one, will return, recharged, with rich vengeance.

3.

Use People

Anthropologists since Virginia's day have rewritten some old myths about a person's potential. They've shown that intelligence is a more social thing than we've assumed. In this model, what you know is not so much the information shut up or *islanded* in your head, but the way you make contact with people around you. We are not wise in a vacuum; instead, we're built by the relationships we manage to make.

Here's a quick example of how knowledge grows through outside connections: Imagine two kids with approximately the same starting IQ. Give one kid skills and access to the Internet. The other only gets to think alone. Ask them to think about global warming, and after ten years, check on their progress. The kid with the Internet access will be able to speak more facts, and connect more important, disparate details, and generally look more versed about the world than the other kid will. What appears to be his "smarts" is also just the extent to which he's tapped his recourses and tied data together into ideas.

The theory here is that we've often thought of intelligence as a too-private thing, assuming we rely on ourselves to look smart. But it's important to remember that we actually change who we are and what we can do in the world by the amount we make contact with others.

A main thinker behind this theory of social identity is the anthropologist Edwin Hutchins. He gives a colorful example of the ship captain in his book *Cognition in the Wild*. When a captain is docking his ship, he uses information that is not just his private store of facts, but the result of whatever communication he manages with his docking team. That is, his ability to do his job has a lot to do with his ability to communicate with the shore. His knowledge as a captain is not locked up in his head, but enacted in the links he forms to the people related to his business.

Knowing this means knowing that creativity is not just a private but a social practice. We see Virginia intuit this idea on a trip to an art collection in 1918. In the first week of April, she went to look at some paintings with her sister and their friend Roger Fry. As they looked at Delacroix and Cézanne, Virginia privately felt her own take on the art. She appreciated Cézanne's apples for "their relationship to each other, and their colour, and their solidity," she wrote in her diary. But then she also realized she was with people who could teach her. Because her sister and Roger Fry were both painters, they saw paintings differently than she did. Virginia could get new insight into painting itself if she asked them what they saw. To Roger and Vanessa, Virginia wrote, the paintings engaged in issues that Virginia could not have imagined on her own. Roger and Vanessa thought in terms "of pure paint or mixed; if pure which colour; emerald or veridian; & then the laying on of the paint; & the time he'd spent, & how he'd altered it, & why, & when he'd painted it."

The idea here: Visiting a museum with a friend who's actually a painter, or seeing a movie with an actor friend, or sitting at a political dinner with an activist friend, can be a chance to step outside of your own professionalized mind-set. Opening up even means lightening the *burden* you feel to understand things on your own. It also means admitting that other people know the world differently than you—and often as well as you do.

Imagine you're watching a play, and you spend the energy to reach some full personal reading or opinion of it. To know more, you should turn to the guy next to you and hold on to also hear what different observations he made. Listening means ingesting that foreign detail, to let it sit and rattle in your mental map of the world. A fresh detail needs time—as a chance to change you.

The idea here is to undo old habits by acknowledging the potential of outside input. An opinion that's new often feels dry, irrelevant, or off-the-mark. But the test is to put your first impulses on hold while you listen with an almost self-silencing flexibility, what John Keats called "negative capability." He meant you need to suppress your own assumptions to digest what's new. Woolf would also add the practical here: Seek out opinions where they've had a chance to really develop, through your well-read friends, an arts center, courses at a college.

4.
Stop Over-Apologizing

"Dinner last night at the Hutchinsons. Let me see. Praise of my dress—taken very philosophically." This is the diary, July 24, 1934. Virginia's suffering after a party again. She's disappointed that when a friend gave her a simple compliment, she took it so critically. Fashion was always a nexus for her neurosis—she never thought she dressed right, didn't like herself in the mirror.

Today, she just wishes she could have taken the compliment with a lighter heart. She should have stood up straight, looked the Hutchinsons in the eye, and simply said "Thank you."

Saying "thank you" is a way of allowing a piece of information to exist, to sit there out in the open. Maybe you are pretty. You've never wanted to admit it. Rejecting a compliment is a way of never accruing debts, never being in the embarrassing position of presenting yourself as more than you are. Escaping compliments means escaping loaded, potentially honest news about you.

A story about how my friend told me he learned about composure: He was in a bad relationship in college. He was particularly moody and would take his emotions out on his girlfriend—bickering about movies, gas, class, the smallest things. After a fight, they'd storm off, but he'd always find the strength to eventually say, "I'm sorry." His responsive girlfriend always appreciated it and routinely accepted him back.

But they were stuck in this cycle, of fighting and apologizing. One day my friend had the feeling that he should stop using "I'm sorry." "Sorry" had become a magical reversal; he was able to get away with anything as long as he had this easy, reliable Band-Aid. So the next few fights meant a longer lingering tension. They had to sit with the *facts* of their fight. But forcing himself to surrender the magic reversal, he said, was the first step to rethinking the moods themselves. When you honestly look at how your behavior upsets other people, you can be motivated to actually change it.

· · · · ·

COMPLIMENTS, LIKE TANTRUMS, ARE real. It might be best not to run from them with language like "I didn't mean it!" or "That's not me!" Be wary of all versions of this: "I would never have done that if . . . !" Certain moments with others give us the chance to see our personalities. Someone can explain a side of you, and the honest words can prompt real change.

Virginia wished she had accepted the Hutchinsons' comment and not giggled it away. She should withstand the discomfort of information—to make it useful.

5.
But Don't Worry Too Much About Change

Sometimes change feels impossible. You think of possible moves, but they're too massive to try. Imagine looking across the room at your seeming-opposite—maybe a documentary filmmaker whose movies have been big enough to actually initiate change in a couple of government policies. In comparison, you feel like you've never been active enough, and you've lived long enough that change seems unlikely.

Comparisons, Woolf writes, can feel paralyzing. We exaggerate types into opposites even when they're not quite that. I name myself with my fictions. "I'm a teacher." This "I" coalesces more tightly in awe of its opposite: "I'm not like that documentary filmmaker." I emphasize my qualities in contrast to hers—in my mind, these two things migrate to their poles. But the fact is, Virginia writes, our definitions of ourselves claim more specificity than they should.

The fact is, you never were just this "teacher-self," and this means that a change in "who I am" might not mean a total uprooting, just an added focus, or a couple of new behaviors tacked onto your routine.

Go to a day in Virginia's life. In the winter of 1926, she went to Berkeley Square to hear a lecture by Tolstoy's daughter. Just peeking over the podium, the hunched Tatiana Tolstoy told the story of her parents—how they ran a school for peasants, were violent in their marriage, raised thirteen children, and how Tolstoy wandered as an ascetic at the end of his life, having finished ninety volumes. Woolf was sitting back in Berkeley Square, with friends whose only hard work that day might have been scribbling away in their notebooks. She looked around at her peers and thought they were all frivolous, as if they had "cheeks of paté de foie gras" and no clue at all what raising thirteen kids during the Russian winters was like, as she wrote in a letter to Vita on January 31, 1926.

After the lecture, Woolf and friends got a cab and went for dinner. Someone promised to introduce Virginia to a woman who had worked for a fashion house in Paris. Woolf felt a cloud come over her. She hated this clash of perspectives: Tolstoy's life cast hers as superficial. "I hated us all, for being prosperous and comfortable; and wished to be a working woman," Woolf wrote in her letter to Vita. The image of hardworking Russians haunted her through dinner—so her friends looked ridiculous and she could only hope for a total shift in position. "I [felt] I didn't want to meet the upper classes," Woolf wrote to Vita. "I wanted to meet washerwomen, and shopkeepers."

Seeing something radically different shook her up. She wanted, like we all want from time to time, to lift her body out of its present situation and history.

· · · · ·

PARALYSIS CAN HAPPEN HERE, when you punish yourself: *How can I convert myself from an upper-middle-class British woman to someone as tough and real as a Russian peasant?* But one thing Virginia would urge is patience. You can remember that change is not always, or ever, an utter revolution.

"The most important thing," Virginia tells herself in her diary on May 17, 1932, "is not to think very much about oneself. To investigate candidly the charge; but not fussily, not very anxiously. On no account to retaliate by going to the other extreme—thinking too much." That is, see the model someone sets. Take advice, or take a cue from experience. But then maybe sleep on it. Don't tighten into some exaggerated definition of identities, and some sob story about self-revision. The actual shift can come in small, practical steps that aren't so hard once the drama diffuses.

If you're a "Miami businesswoman," you're also other women—someone who's been to certain parts of the world, or had other interests, or thinks in ways not all businesswomen do. Talents have always been developing under the radar. In that spirit, Woolf resolved that she didn't have to *become* Tatiana Tolstoy. She would, of course, go on being Woolf (which is unique and valuable), and maybe just add elements about social class to her next book. She could write more about the tension between working class and aristocracy. Obviously the interest was already in her. The shift to new behavior doesn't mean erasing what you've done and starting from zero.

One more example: I used to have a little rule that *I'm not a movie person*. It saved time and money. I called myself a "reader." This way, I didn't have to deal with movie decisions.

Recently, I went to a movie and loved it. Sadly enough, I felt a *biting* pang afterward: *I've missed out all this time! Idiot—I've been valuing reading as if it's so much different. I've missed out on too much.*

I probably feared some total change. *Now I'll have to go to so many movies!* But the fear was silly. It was self-whipping. The truth is I'll go to a few more movies. Not a *new* me, just some added activity that puts a new layer on my identity.

· · · · ·

VIRGINIA REMINDS US OF the habits we have, and of ways to move from one routine to a new one. She says that routines are hard to break, but sometimes worth fiddling with. One self resists change, but change is reviving. We can throw ourselves into new cycles when the old ones have run out of fuel.

CHAPTER 11

Read Your Partner

LET'S GO BACK TO the novels—and to relationships. We make a common mistake about human nature when we claim that we always at least have the *choice* to say what we mean. It's not that we don't want to say what we mean, but our emotions do have a tendency toward a nasty double-speak. When I say something like, "The Red Sox will win the Series" or "It'll rain," I often mean another thing, like, "I know more about the world than you do." Sentences are not just vessels of facts, but reflections of what we feel and want, a code for what we cannot say.

Woolf is history's master at showing our emotions to be

the puppeteers behind our language, the directors behind even mundane conversations. She says that unspoken needs direct us—and we'll get the most out of our conversations if we can understand the way our interactions work.

· · · · ·

IN *TO THE LIGHTHOUSE,* Woolf gets inside relationships in a more revealing way than she does anywhere else. The novel is largely about gender relationships—about the roles Woolf sees men and women take in the world. Of course Virginia grew up in the late Victorian era, so the gender roles she knew were more distinctly polarized than they are today. But she paints a dynamic we can still understand—both in and out of the roles we take as men and women. In essence, Woolf gave us a man in the book who's pretty strong but narcissistic: He poses as proud of himself, but he's actually highly dependent on the awe that others (here: his wife) give him.

The woman in the book plays a different role, as silent and underappreciated helpmate. She's her husband's audience and stage hand, listening on to what he says and offering the support he's asking for. Though she often sees how pathetic he is, she's still committed to her role. This is partly because she's generous, but it's also because she has her own vanity issues: She only feels safe when she's in the presence of a partner who looks, at least, in control.

In the opening scene of *To the Lighthouse*, we meet Mrs. Ramsay sitting in her window seat, knitting. Her six-year-old son, James, is playing at her feet, cutting pictures out of a magazine. He's excited to go sailing with Dad tomorrow, to the lighthouse.

Dad's on the porch outside, pacing. He's in serious mode—in a conversation with his protégée, his student from Oxford. But while he performs as mentor, Dad is also worried about how important he actually is to other people. At heart, he's always worried about this. His intellectual bravado does only so much to shore up his pride, "the land dwindling away . . . pathetically small, half swallowed up in the sea," as Mr. Ramsay thinks, of the beach they live on if not directly of himself.

So, at a pause in this conversation with his student, Dad pokes his head through the living room window, where his only pure dependents—his son and wife—are sitting. As he does, we see wheels turning, the power surge in his eyes, his excitement: He sees a quick shot to feeling strong. Perhaps jiggling change in his pocket, touching the edge of the window, Dad smiles at his son and launches small talk: *It's going to rain tomorrow*, he says. *We won't sail to the lighthouse after all.*

On the surface, this seems like casual family conversation, about the weather. But when she sinks us into each player's head in this scene, Woolf also makes it clear that Dad is flattening his son's hopes for tomorrow as a parade of power. For James, the small talk is a shot to the heart. Maybe letting his toy scissors dangle in his lap, James looks up at Dad, feeling deflated, dependent, and too young to say any of it. Mom also stings with regret.

Here Woolf is looking at the feelings that boil under our most casual lines of conversation. The basic idea is that almost everything we say is powered by an emotional desire. Dad talks about the rain, but only because by doing it he can touch or control his son. I say what I say for its covert emotional payoff.

In turn, Woolf says we need to look at the unspoken emotions whenever we want to make a conversation work. The better I am at reading between the lines when we talk, the better I am at controlling my demands, attending to others' needs, and then even getting what I want. We see this in the novel when, after Mr. Ramsay's word about the weather, Woolf drops us into his wife's perspective.

When Mrs. Ramsay sees her husband dash their son's dreams about tomorrow's trip, she's frustrated. She sees his arrogance, his inability to fully and directly express himself. In turn, she basically sees two options. One option is to call his attention to it, saying something like, "Don't be a jerk to your son." This would be like telling a needy friend (imagine a friend who's going on and on with his Red Sox stats) to get real: "If you want attention, *ask* for it." You know that sometimes-dire need: You want to tug the line of language taut—*to get everyone to say what's behind the small talk.* But getting anxious about the so-called Truth often leads directly to a fight. If Mrs. Ramsay were to assert her ego, slap her man and say, "Speak straight!" Mr. Ramsay would probably sense the attack and just defend himself: "But *it is* going to rain." He'd check the barometer to bolster his side (which he actually does do in the novel). In her own knee jerk, Mrs. Ramsay might spit: "How do you *know?*" Now you see these two are already coming close to what we'd call the classic, stupid bicker: They lock horns about rain predictions while really referring to power.

· · · · ·

THE OTHER OPTION MRS. RAMSAY has is to slow down—to just surrender to this sad fact that we all talk in code. She can admit our limits: that we've got emotional needs that we can't always translate into daily language. She doesn't beat her husband up for it.

In this scenario, she'd see what her husband *implies,*

and, without showing off her own store of facts, actually give him some of what he's asking for. She sees he's a deluded partner, but she doesn't assume that she, herself, is so much more honest, self-aware, or altruistic. (She knows she also often talks in code.) So she loosens up a little— *lets* her lover ask for respect while he pretends to talk about the weather.

This coded communication isn't ideal, of course. We'd like it more if people had the self-knowledge and courage to speak their needs directly—for Mr. and Mrs. Ramsay to be self-aware and direct. I'd like to read and live scenes with sentences that show calm composure: "I need to feel supported right now," or "I need your respect." But Woolf doesn't serve up ideal relationships as much as real ones— and in describing these scenes, she's still able to highlight the noblest parts. We get rich humanity, for instance, when Mrs. Ramsay is able to read her husband's needs without getting unhinged with bitterness. As the plot moves along, she lets Mr. Ramsay talk about the weather, stomachs her own impulse to bicker, and then helps her son deal with this (albeit ugly) situation by giving him a new, distracting game to play.

Mrs. Ramsay's good at the dance we simply have to do to keep relationships together. She isn't brilliant or baldly honest, but she makes up for a lot of that with humility;

she can let the other guy "be right" from time to time; she's cool enough to provide the thing he doesn't name. She's big enough to even cater, at times, to hypocrisy. Mrs. Ramsay values humane feelings more than factual accuracy in her life.

· · · · ·

As I said in an earlier chapter, I'm in training as a psychologist—and what's interesting is that the message Woolf delivers here, about reading between the lines with people we care about, is also a focus point in clinical training. A good listener needs to be highly attuned to what's said in the *manner*, and not just the facts, of speaking; we get to new places by reading what our conversation partners don't yet have the power to say.

Take an example: Someone comes into your office, uptight. He sweats in his chair, knits his brow, speaks in pressured sentences. A couple of times when you try to make a suggestion, he leans forward to challenge your perspective: "Wrong. *That's not it.*" He's disagreeing all the time—but to ask him to change that stance, you've got to acknowledge its code. He doesn't simply, consistently think you're factually incorrect; instead he's communicating a mood. He wants control. This fact about him means he'd just *fight back* if you pushed for your own perspective right now. Instead—in the beginning at least—just receive what he *means*; focus on what he's asking. Let him talk; sit back in your chair; listen. At least then the guy knows you *can hear* the unspoken message, about control. If he trusts you understand how to listen like that (and note: his "understanding" that you're listening isn't so conscious—it's really just relaxation), he might also eventually trust you've got something worthwhile to add to this dialogue. You read the hidden demands, and that sense of dialogue is precisely what breaks the deadlock.

· · · · ·

WE HAVE THE ABILITY, and responsibility, to hear what people mean but aren't saying. We get kind when we respond with the needed elements. No one just talks with facts. In this sense, we need to work with conversation like a dance: You slow the pace by slowing down your own *movements* rather than immediately firing back, defensively, with surface-driven language.

Words communicate with a *how*, not just a *what*, Woolf says. Mrs. Ramsay allows her husband to vent—and that's how she steps in stride with him. We don't always want to play this game, the dance. Sometimes it's better to speak straight. But the more we know about how language works, the less reactive we are, and the more strategic we can be. Woolf urges us to humility—to admit we're not always straight with talk or self-knowledge, and shouldn't demand others always be, either.

CHAPTER 12

Make Use of Time

ONE OF VIRGINIA'S MAJOR fascinations was with what she called the "moment"—the seconds that pass unacknowledged. As she once wrote to Vita, large-scale love is boring, and "the excitement of life lies in the 'little moves' nearer to people." Interest lies in the hints and implications we exchange.

Woolf's focus on the moment came largely in the vein of other philosophers in her time—from Walter Pater to phenomenologists like Martin Heidegger—who were kicking against an older philosophical tradition that valued unmovable facts about reality. In place of that, Woolf focused on ever-changing, passing moments. She wanted to bring her microscope to what these moments of experience *felt* like—how contradictory emotions, antithetical impulses, maybe mania, self-doubt, and memory, all come at us at once.

Woolf's fascination was with the way daily life runs up against memory or longing. In her memoir "A Sketch of the Past," she describes just how she feels when history flavors the present: A memory begins, and only then "one sees through the surface to the depths. In those moments I find one of my greatest satisfactions, not that I am thinking of the past; but that it is then that I am living most fully in the present. For the present when backed by the past is a thousand times deeper than the present when it presses so close that you can feel nothing else, when the film on the camera reaches only the eye." This is the focus of much of her writing: She loves how our moments are full when we're not just watching life, as if watching a mere picture show, but making connections through memories. Then life's layered.

So for Woolf, life is rich when we're thinking on several levels—dealing with old and new, joy and fear. Go to the everyday: You're sitting in your office. Everything feels humdrum. You look across the desk. If you're bored, you want a better sense of texture. You'd like, perhaps, to feel that the second you're living is loaded like a firecracker. Something's inside it. But at the desk, you don't quite *feel* the potential. Habit weighs down. You laugh at the inaccessibility of the Zen koan on the day counter: *Every moment contains the now.*

One of the central goals of Woolf's fiction is to magnify the small moments to reveal the tension and energy inside them. That's how scenes in her fiction often get their power: We zoom into the pulse of those "little moves," as she named them with Vita, to trace the feelings at work.

· · · · ·

OF COURSE, IT'S HARD to feel potent about time. For one, boredom is boredom. Boredom is actually that large shadow that sweeps over whole parts of our day but we don't usually name. Boredom is forgettable, killing whole portions of our lives without our noticing. It's what Virginia called the "non-being" hours in her memoir "A Sketch of the Past." She wrote that life is, for the most part, interesting, but our "moments of being [are] embedded in many more moments of non-being. . . . When it is a bad day the proportion of non-being is much larger." For Woolf, non-being happened when the mind was disengaged, without the energy or assertiveness for interpreting things. She also called that time "cotton wool," which is like a brain fog. She claimed that her job as an artist was to occasionally jump out of cotton wool to touch what's real and vibrant behind monotony. For Woolf, mindlessness glued much of life together, but was as sad as it was central: dead time for the living.

· · · · ·

To take the technical turn here, know that boredom is assuming a larger role in psychiatry these days. Scientists have been studying boredom as one of those important elements in life that goes unnoticed, but sits behind larger setbacks we do notice, like relapses in a mental illness or alcohol addiction. Researchers have argued that we need to study boredom more, because even though we've often ignored it as the simple, innocuous downtime, the mood is actually a trigger behind some of our biggest acknowledged problems, from drug relapse to mental illness.

We basically know what boredom is—the feeling that nothing's happening while time passes. The psychologist McWelling Todman published one definition of boredom in his study of its role in addiction and schizophrenia by calling boredom an inability to "give perspective and meaning to the routine activities of life (i.e. fantasy, anticipation, etc.).'" He's talking about the inability to turn a dazed passivity into a fact that moves you. He's saying that overcoming boredom is being able to turn a daydream into something solid, an activity that changes the flow of time to solid deeds—like a hobby or a business.

· · · · ·

STEP BACK AND SEE how hard it is to snap from a wash of time to actually building a potent life. I remember recently lying back on my bed and leafing through an old diary. I heard the cars passing by on the street, with nothing to do that day. I had my foot on my bent knee, and drank tea. Leafing through, I found the entry from the day I finished my English doctoral degree. That day, I'd handed in the dissertation to the office secretary, then walked through the grass to the park, eating a hot dog. I'd called my mother. We'd made plans for dinner. By ten I'd set my alarm and gone to bed. I now remembered the vague feeling of the day, where no one moment had special *meaning*. The day had passed as what Woolf called cotton wool. At no point during that day did I stop to feel *I am living a turning point*. Reading the diary now, I had a feeling of loss, like the day had slipped by without some celebration it deserved. At the end of my life, if there were some summing up of my high points, that day would probably be one of them, but I hadn't had the intuition to know the moment as it passed. Somehow, the afternoon had been a wash.

· · · · ·

WHY? WOOLF'S MAIN EXPLANATION for how this happens is that no moment comes with a reason why it matters. After finishing my PhD, I didn't feel just one emotion named "happy." Woolf makes a big point of this: You can easily get lost in a moment because no emotion comes on its own. It locks horns with others. I probably felt good about being done, but guilty for not editing the dissertation better. I remember I'd felt fat and full from a big lunch. I was worried about the new problem of finding a job as a teacher. I hoped bigger things were still in my future. I didn't think the moment I was *in* was worth calling extraordinary. That's a function of guilt, a flimsy confidence, and a lack of a sense of *fun.*

Woolf was fascinated with how conflicting emotions can carry any moment from a solid thing into a less definitive gray. She shows this in "Together and Apart," a story in which a woman sits next to a man on a couch and wants to love, "but directly the word 'love' occurred to her, she rejected it, thinking again how obscure the mind was, with its very few words for all these astonishing perceptions, these alternations of pain and pleasure. For how did one name this. That is what she felt now, the withdrawal of human affection." The character finds it hard to say "love." Emotions don't come one at a time.

Even at an anniversary or New Year's party, it's hard to feel *we're here*. Looking across a table at your long-term lover, it's hard to think *this is the biggest relationship, and one of the biggest moments in it, that I will have*. That's only because there are doubts and their counterpoints.

. . . . .

WOOLF WAS, GRANTED, UTTERLY in love with the ambiguity of that wash. She even thought the power of the moment depended on this complexity—the way memory clashes with action, where one emotion jams up against another. But she was also aware of how dangerous it is to sink into non-being, and claimed that her challenge as a writer was to receive some *shock*, then to arrive at a statement. When "I receive these sudden shocks," she wrote in her memoir "A Sketch of the Past," "they are now always welcome; after the first surprise, I always feel instantly that they are particularly valuable. And so I go on to suppose that the shock-receiving capacity is what makes me a writer."

How to turn a washy day after writing a dissertation into the party rush it should be? See me on my bed while reading my diary. I'd come to my first realization: that some moments had passed in my life, and I hadn't snapped out of my dream state to embrace them. Here I was again, on my bed. How to feel that even this moment—which felt as mundane as every single moment feels—was memorable? One thing I needed to do was to claim more importance than I tended to. Even Proust, Flaubert, and Abraham Lincoln, in history, felt mundane in ordinary moments. The difference is, they had the guts to call themselves creative, and then to take the small steps to making something. It takes claiming your potential to start a project.

You need to become the famous person other people write about—to know your potential rides in a moment that feels almost completely mundane. To see this, find Woolf on one of her own boring days, in early October 1917. She was wandering around her house, then opened a cupboard and found a box with a dusty notebook in it. She brushed it off, seeing a diary she'd tried to keep two years before. She'd written in it every day from January 1 to February 2, 1915, but then had let it trail off. Now she sat down in her chair and flipped through it. She read some passages about a friend. *My God*, she thought, *this is funnier than I thought*. She had the strange feeling that two years ago, she'd actually been writing good stuff, and hadn't appreciated it while it had been going on. Some descriptions she'd written of her friend Walter Lamb made her laugh. What a gas—she'd been doing interesting work but hadn't ever thought it. So she started a new diary on that day, October 8, 1917:

> This attempt at a diary is begun on the impulse given by the discovery in a wooden box in my cupboard of an old volume, kept in 1915, & still able to make us laugh at Walter Lamb. This therefore will follow that plan— written after tea, written indiscreetly, & by the way L[eonard] has promised to add his page when he has something to say. . . . We planned today to get him an autumn outfit in clothes, & to stock me with paper & pens. This is the happiest day that exists for me. It rained steadily of course. London seems unchanged.

That was October 8. Virginia opened up her book and saw that an old self had produced something witty and not acknowledged the productivity at the time. So she put her foot in the ground—*I'm going to start a productive routine.* It would be stupid to wait for a day in which she knew more, had more talent, or was more worthy. Washington wasn't perfect when he rallied his troops at Yorktown.

She and Leonard rushed into town and got her pens. When they got home, to the patter of rain, Leonard put his clothes away, and she started to write on the first page of the diary.

This one day's decision was the beginning of one of the most famous and highly read diaries in history. One morning, she knew that what some people would one day call "history in the making" feels like a gray wash to the hero doing the action. It's fun to see how small and simple the moment was for her: *Today*, she said, *I'll get myself pens*. "This is the happiest day that exists for me." She stuck her stake in the ground, turning wash into action.

Go back to the psychologist Dr. Todman. He said the chronic sort of boredom that leads to unlivable lives is an inability to turn passing moments into personally meaningful moments. Certain contexts and illnesses will, of course, be bigger than we are. But ordinary life also threatens to smother you, too. Here, boredom is a lack of creativity and self-reliance. Woolf was able to convert a moment quite simply, by saying *I'm good enough*, and then picking an activity to start. She narrows the gap between herself and the Greats this way. Remember that every Great had to convince herself to crack ambiguity, simply by knowing she could. Memorable things start like this: an ordinary person convinces herself she has potential, then picks up the phone to begin a committee, to plan a party or rent a performance space; she opens a page and starts.

CHAPTER 13

Read and Be More

WE ALL KNOW THE value of reading. It's comfort and an accessible escape. Reading does seem to have shifted outside of the center of today's public culture, where movies and the Internet dominate the landscape. But books have so far been able to survive the cultural shift because they do offer a game that's specific to what they are. In Woolf's opinion, novels made unique requirements of the mind, challenging us to find empathy with the author, patience with grasping tone and plot, creativity in supplying images to words, and dexterity in following the author's, rather than your own, assumptions. We read, she wrote in "How Should One Read a Book?" "not to throw light on literature, not to become familiar with famous people, but to refresh and exercise our own creative powers." Below are reasons how and why books, unlike quite anything else in the world, push us.

1.

Reading Makes Me Silly

Reading is a good test of attention; it's also a great way to exercise an inattentive dance of your own. Reading can be a chance for a daydream, fuel for your own thinking.

My first year in college, my ambition was big, and I wasn't scared by how much had already been done and thought in history. I didn't know enough to be scared. I wanted to be a writer; I loved digging into difficult books.

When I read Plato in Philosophy 101, I fell in love. I took him to the woods; I read him on walks. I sometimes misread him—running with his words, thinking faster on my own. He seemed like he'd gotten away with so much—played with logic like clay. He'd state one argument that seemed to be true, but then extend it just a bit, then again, daringly, until he ended an argument in a ridiculous position, like "All people love Truth equally." I laughed at how he led us through that carnival maze to a silly place, playing on words. I gripped the book and walked around the woods, feeling *thought is art*. I was high—felt I understood the tricks he was doing, and could one day be an artist/philosopher, too.

Even then, I knew I was misreading some parts of Plato—that I could sit down, grant his logic more credit, understand his different historical perspective, and try to follow the text more faithfully. But that wasn't so much the point at that time. I was using Plato to psych myself up to think artistically. Not utterly honest to the text, I was using it; his work gave me energy. It spun enough tricks to make me feel capable of building my own ideas.

· · · · ·

You're going to misread some people, and you (loving your head) are going to relish the thoughts that come from the misreading. Woolf indulged this fact. She reads not by "seeking meaning [but] rather [by] letting [myself] run on for pleasure, [this] is . . . my way, & thus naturally richest and best," she wrote in her diary in September 1918. She meant reading is one catalyst for your own creative trip. Sometimes you read for just half the idea; sometimes you'll finish a paragraph and realize you didn't digest a single word of it. The book can be a background song to your thinking.

Reading can be the world's best prod to your own creativity, she'd say. Think of the parallel in our spoken conversations: We're not always as faithful to the other person's thought as we could be. But that's not a sin—it's how two heads work simultaneously. You say something, and I kind of get it, but I'm already forming my response in my head. I'm doing it to bounce off you, and to add a piece of my own. Although conversation, Woolf would say, is primarily a chance to hear how *another* person thinks, it's also the plain old place we feel inspired and primed to add elements that interest us.

We talk to jump off other voices. Books might be the best stage for this joyful creative misreading, because books contain someone's most challenging ideas, and they don't get offended or bully you back onto track as you leave them for your own direction. You drop them into your lap, stare into space, choose your own pace, indulge your own train of thought—even drop the book altogether, and get writing. A book is a playful conversation that doesn't mind being just a spark for your own unexpected responses.

Plato meant what he wrote (and later I would read him in a more academic way), but in the park he was a partner telling me I could be an artist I hadn't thought of being before.

2.

But: Reading to Communicate with Other People

It's a lovely thing to read something twisted and pounce to your own ideas, or to construe your next sentence when someone talks. But Woolf is also interested in the flip side, which is a bigger part of maturity: She's interested in how we can put ourselves aside to actually *listen* to other people.

That skill also gets developed by reading. Virginia called reading a challenge of empathy, a time in which you're asked to stop galloping with ideas—to turn down your loves and assumptions long enough to follow a narrative, which is someone else's world perspective. Reading well means entering a different head, or even a different century. The memoirs of a monk in 1440 are probably your one chance to really sit in the seat from which his 1440 logic and values *functioned*. You get to move the ways his eyes go, and, as you read him, you have to find the empathy for his tone to "get" his perspective.

Books—one here, one there, voices through human history—are the sort of disembodied party space where dead, living, and far-off minds convene. See someone sitting

168 § A Life of One's Own

with her dog-eared copy of Aristotle in a bar right off
the docks in Biloxi. Water's making music on the bellies of
boats. When the woman reads her uncle's college notes in
the margins of her book, she knows he also held this book
somewhere, like this, in some other place and year. She
drinks her beer and feels thrilled with all the heads at this
party. She's drinking with a Greek philosopher, her uncle,
and her cousin, who also read this book a few years ago.
They've all spent time in the same viewpoint of this book.

Woolf gives us a glimpse of this cruising literary party
in a scene in her novel *The Years*, when a young Edward
Pargiter sits at his desk for his first year away at Oxford. His
dad's mailed him a case of port to celebrate the beginning
of his academic journey, and as he opens the play *Antigone*,
Edward feels this sweetness of history, of how all people,
from the beginning of language, have made resonating at-
tempts to think through the same old scenery. He feels the
responsibility of appreciating tradition, and really wants to
get it when he reads. He licks his pen and digs in: "Little
negligible words now revealed shades of meaning which
altered the meaning. He made another note; *that* was the
meaning," Woolf writes in the novel. "He must be precise;
exact. . . . He must let nothing dwindle off into vagueness."
He follows the book to connect with what's come before,
feeling joy at the responsibility of being human.

He opens his dad's port and drinks. That's what books deliver: History at your fingertips.

But you don't want to just sit idle and witness it, Virginia goes on. She thinks the excitement of tapping into this record of human footsteps should remind you of your individual interpretation of things.

The play Edward's reading, *Antigone*, happens to be a tragedy in which a child feels demoralized and overlooked by her father's law. Antigone is basically a woman who—though she'll soon be the king's daughter-in-law—feels out of step with tradition. Her brother died when fighting the city, and though Antigone wants to bury him, the king's law won't allow her to do it. The play traces her effort to find some place that's both authentic to her actual feelings and respectful of authority.

Woolf's character Edward is doing the same thing as he reads: He is, after all, this nervous, individual, boyish guy in an Oxford dorm. He's not Sophocles or Aristotle or his tutors or his father. He wants to read for the book's true intention, but he also feels the challenge to find his own place in the human conversation—to stage his own quirky, rebellious voice. This is the clash between individual insight and public record. You get to your freshman year at college, for example, and hear you're supposed to love Shakespeare. You don't first feel like you do. But being a "good reader" is also a test: How much can you tone down your first impressions to try to understand the author's context beside other voices? You need to be patient to take history in. Only after patience comes the funner self-assertion: You have to add something, by writing a paper or responding to the book. You respect that others have something to say, then offer your fire by speaking up. Woolf's Edward finds his voice by publishing his own poetic translation of *Antigone*. This is Woolf's sign that he's grown into an adult: He spends the energy to listen to people before him, then interacts by offering his own voice.

That's actually lesson number one in teaching essay writing to students: You have to grapple with an author's context before staging your own creative critique. We have to listen to other voices before responding to them.

If you go further, you see that this idea behind faithful reading is tied to all other types of good communication, even dating. The first challenge on a date with someone who has a radically different head from yours is toning down your knee-jerk instincts. A good listener silences first defenses to *listen*. A dynamic partner tries to get inside the narrative the other person spins. You have to be flexible about the new before you can judge or, better, like it.

The big challenge in reading, as in listening to any new voice, is withholding the quickest first judgments—then dancing with your partner's word into your own reflective turn.

3.

Makes You Moral, Too

Books can also make you patient.

The dad Mr. Ramsay in *To the Lighthouse* gets depressed after his dinner party. At dinner, he hears a guest say that the great novelist Sir Walter Scott is irrelevant, and it bugs him, haunting him as he strolls to the living room after dessert. That's because Ramsay has always considered *himself* a great thinker, and he's imagined that if his work parallels anyone's in history, it's Scott's. Unable to shake this insecurity, he strolls to his bookshelf and picks up a Scott novel to read. He wants to re-establish what greatness is, and isn't.

In general, Ramsay tends toward depression because he's rigid about his self-description as *intelligent* and thinks that intelligence itself is a stiff, unforgiving thing. You either have it or you don't, and this tense notion about personal value makes him competitive with others. For Ramsay intelligence runs in a line that allows you to rate all participants—"like the alphabet . . . twenty-six letters all in order. . . . [Ramsay] reached Q. . . . Q he was sure of. Q he could demonstrate. If Q then is Q—R—. Here he knocked his pipe out, with two or three resonant taps on the handle of the urn, and proceeded. 'Then R . . .' He braced himself. He clenched himself," Woolf writes in the novel. He feels strapped to the challenge of *proving* his genius, and the pressure makes him aggressive when he thinks of himself in a public context.

A mere dinner comment sinks him into silence.

But when Ramsay picks up Scott's actual book from his shelf, he re-encounters a major gift of reading. Books show us how textured a mind is. Reading reminds us of the essence of creativity: that we're too different to be rated on a scale from A to Z.

A book shows you a personality in performance, a landscape of emotion and images. (It's a parade, which is why I hate the reductive question, "Who's your favorite author?") If Sir Walter Scott dances in a complex and remarkable way in his book, that doesn't change or decrease the things that Ramsay can do. Two big thinkers are different but both interesting.

Seeing this allows Ramsay to relax a little, as if you realize you don't have to run to the supermarket to get the last cheese on sale. Other sales happen on other days. Open your notebook and be *yourself*. The book simply "fortified him. . . . Now, he felt, it didn't matter a damn who reached Z (if thought ran like an alphabet from A to Z). Somebody would reach it—if not he, then another." Seeing that art is someone's expression, he feels less desperate to compete with his colleagues. A good novel reminds him of what it is to think originally: doing what you do, persistently, not only for outdoing others.

Woolf's getting us to see that good work is earnest work. Ramsay relaxes when he sees that Scott won fame because he deserved it. He sees a larger, more generous playing field for expression. One person's success is a deep self-expression, and it doesn't use up the ways you can also be honest and big. So Ramsay sees what he's got to do, and it's a more pleasant task: Listen to yourself; dare to do something with it; edit. Making a new business or art takes patience—so Ramsay reminds himself to find the same authentic relationship to his own personality.

Coda

One literary critic has written beautifully about this idea. Lawrence Lipking wrote a piece about Mary Shelley's *Frankenstein*, describing why it's a useful thing to study literature. Literature, he said, is a good chance to deal with the ambiguity that's utterly human. Math and science ask for clarity—to boil down the seeming chaos in the galaxy to the laws that govern it. Science is a wonderful and useful art in that sense, the task of drawing a black and white from the mess. But literature asks for a different skill. Reading demands humility, where we sit with something uncomfortable rather than rushing to name it. In *Frankenstein*, we get a main character with a big heart, but who still ends up hurting people he loves. The story brings on ethical questions: Did Frankenstein do something *wrong*? His intentions were as good as he could manage. So what should he have done differently? But the memorable thing about the text is that it doesn't give a simple answer to the paradox. It gets you to admit the discomforting fact that good motivations often lead to bad conclusions. Literature demands we just *face* something threatening, and the ethics of that exercise are simple: I endure what is unlike me, without bolting to impose a rule about what "should" happen.

4.

Reading as Peacemaking

There might be no more fraught, long famous marriage than that between Leo Tolstoy and Sofia Andreevna

Tolstaya. In almost fifty years of marriage, they had a lot to negotiate. He was an obsessive, violent man and needed time to write his ninety volumes. She could also get violent when she felt ignored. But there were certain times in their life when they were able to find a groove—to work side by side. She wrote diaries with almost as much self-protective passion as he wrote books.

I might only be imagining one afternoon in 1880, in which they overcame the last night's battle with a retreat to a mutual, parallel pleasure. They took rocking chairs to opposite sides of their porch in Yasnaya Poliana, opened their books, and simply read and wrote, diverging, in peace, in that Russian spring. Here were two people who abused each other and had affairs; they often hated to talk to each other. So books were their sure escape. Words are a place where you can slip away. You're still married to this complex person in the real world, but reading side by side can be the clearest example of how we remain close to, yet escape from, each other every day.

In Woolf's *To the Lighthouse*, the Ramsays find a viable intimacy through distance; they read to bridge their differences . . . by avoiding them. Mr. and Mrs. Ramsay are a married couple who don't always agree. But they often choose to avoid talking about it. They can handle tension by sitting side by side with some hobby—and a handy hobby is reading. Mrs. Ramsay scans poems for their music, and Mr. Ramsay studies something academic. So the brains run fast and happy in parallel but don't have to bristle against each other. "They had nothing to say," Woolf writes, "but something seemed, nevertheless, to go from him to her." An imagined connection happens. They deal with difference by pursuing silent parallel goals.

Books offer that activity that all relationships need: You escape the inflexible with fantasy. In relationships and in literature, humans have the capacity to do this. Good.

See people in jail, spending all the silence reading. See lovers in a spat turning from the fight to their books. They're not turning away from human society altogether. No. They're turning to its most thought-through pulp: the digested (edited, deep, solitary) thoughts of books. See books lift depressed people out of isolation with the sign of authors' solitary work.

Mr. Ramsay knows the solace of books: "Don't interrupt me, he seemed to be saying, don't say anything; just sit there. And he went on reading," Woolf writes. Mrs. Ramsay can also fantasize joy as long as silence lasts. "How satisfying!" her book of poems feels to her. "How restful! . . . Her mind felt . . . clean."

"She had not said it: yet he knew," Woolf writes. Married

people accept human distance by turning to separate, thoughtful hobbies.

Of course that's cynical. And Woolf did want this couple to have a closer connection in that scene—to have the guts to talk—but she's no idealist about how humans interact. We connect and don't connect; where we don't connect, we tend to fill up the gaps with what we want to see. That's precisely the exercise we're asked to perform in reading, too, where there are gaps between words. We have to fabricate the pictures for the words, build the logical links from sentence to sentence, and give the right pace to the book. We fill up the gaps with our imaginative fancy.

So both books and good relationships depend on this ability to bridge gaps with information we make up. Here's peace: Watch your lover work from behind and enjoy the back of his collar, how smart the top of his head looks. You love the idealized gloss of your partner's brilliance, and . . . *get by*. That's what the Tolstoys did throughout their lives—interacted often and joyfully but also found activities for stepping away from an impasse. They had detached personal hobbies they loved.

This need for privacy is partly why actual physical distance makes the heart grow fonder. When your lover's traveling, the imagination does great work to enhance your connection to each other, as if turning life's slop into a nicer novel. "How odd it is—the effect geography has on the mind!" Woolf wrote in a letter to Vita on April 13, 1926. "I write to you differently now you're coming back [from her four month trip from Persia to Poland]. The pathos is melting. I felt it pathetic when you were going away; as if you were sinking below the verge. Now that you are rising, I'm jolly again." My lover's gone to Paris. How I love him and want him back! What's even sweeter: I don't have to say it. I lie quietly in my bed thinking of things, not even picking up the phone to call him.

We misread lovers by filling gaps with fantasy, and do the same with the books we love, even imagining the authors think more *like us* than they really do. You should know that in my own book here, for instance, I'm misreading Woolf on a million points, but because she's not here to correct me, and because my misreadings create a Woolf that's almost my double, my love for her feels vaulted and perfect.

Books lend silence to a relationship, and can be near-perfect lovers for their readers.

5.

Loving Bad Books

A writer in my building struggles with writer's block, and when she does, she goes for a weekend away with what she calls her Bad Books. They're books that aren't fabulous. She can tell where the author struggles to create a scene. She can see the author's personality peeping through the prose. She can laugh at where the book isn't working. But they also energize her more than masterpieces like *War and Peace* because they show that thin membrane between having a funny thought and building art.

Books that are historically fabulous can paralyze her. Sometimes reading a bad book reminds her that she's equally capable of expression, that a plot or idea isn't blocked by a ceiling. Woolf agrees, writing in "Hours in a Library," that when bad books sprawl, they show imagination in its most excited undoctored state. "We owe a great deal to bad books," she writes. They "play so large a part in our silent life"—because they remind us that even great authors can think as sloppily—or as flailingly or simply—as we do. The characters in a bad book "generally end by becoming, for the time at least, actors in those private dramas with which we beguile our solitary walks and our sleepless hours," Woolf writes. She means we feel close to these half-formed worlds because, behind them, we hear their authors struggling to make them.

Bad books remind you that you can turn passing ideas into bigger performances. They don't carry that stifling aura you feel when you read a masterpiece—or visit a monument, or drink a "fine wine"—that's weighted with public admiration. In her essay "On Being Ill," Woolf writes how it's sometimes liberating to be less than successful or—to put it bluntly—sick with the flu: to lie in bed without the energy to either speak or accept the usual clichés, like "I've got to get to work," and "I should be kind to that person over there." When you're sick, you fall out of the busy daily fury; you sometimes even hallucinate against the warping ceiling or imagine voices fluctuating between loud and soft outside the bedroom door. What's better: You're *allowed* to fall out of line, to do the unpolished and unexpected. In some ways, sickness is freedom; in the same way, bad (unhealthy, ill-formed) books broadcast their own liberation. They crumble in parts; they fail to follow through on the promises they make in their beginnings. So Woolf often applauded the bad. She said that at least unhealthy books fly and burn in some pioneering arch instead of running along the same well-worn tracks. They're what's left of old noble efforts.

That is, most of what we do is imperfect, so you've got to feel sweetened in the soul when you see imperfect artifacts others gave us. Half-successful things mark an unchartered horizon and the beating, banging hearts that tried to reach it.

6.
Reading for Fuel

Her death came, close to World War II. Before Woolf killed herself, she read and wrote in a fury, trying to remind herself that human history was respectable—complicated but engaged. She wanted earnest personalities around her. "It's a good thing to have books to believe in," she wrote to Ethel in May 1940. "D'you know what I find?—reading a whole poet is consoling." She read all of Coleridge's work, burying herself in an interesting mind. Then she bought Shelley's works, also "to explore [him] in the same sauntering under the bramble way." She told Ethel that because significance in the outside world was growing thin, she needed this escape.

Books are a dependable voice of humor and curiosity. Woolf planned a massive last writing project, too: a tour through all of English literature, a review of her reading life. As Hitler's bombs fell on London, Virginia kept reading and writing to bolster her sense of self. "I've written you ever so many beautiful letters," she writes to Ethel two months before her death, "cigarette letters—you know the kind. . . . These are the letters I write you, about 3 on a wet windy morning. . . . Extend your lighthouse Beam over this dark spot and tell me what you see." More: "Did I tell you I'm reading the whole of English literature through? By the time I've reached Shakespeare the bombs will be falling. So I've arranged a very nice last scene: reading Shakespeare, having forgotten my gas mask, I shall fade away, and quite forget. . . . They brought down a raider the other side of Lewes yesterday. . . . Thank God, as you would say, one's fathers left one a taste for reading! . . . I think, only three months to read Ben Jonson, Milton, Donne, and all the rest!"

Her reference to the "lighthouse Beam" shows how she tries to step out of her books to actual friendships in the world. She's using one of her own literary metaphors, for common talk: Send your thinking this way, Ethel; talk to me, she says.

She contrasts the anxiety of real friendship with the

safety of books. That image of the lighthouse beam is her symbol for how fractured contact is: We live with a routine hit-and-miss, cycles of disappointment like when the lighthouse beam is occluded. Human generosity—especially in war time—is also inconsistent. In turn, books offered Virignia a contrasting constant light, an ongoing conversation, a static model of purpose.

But books are not detached or outside of human life; they're images that suggest ways to live. At the end of her letter to Ethel, Virginia manages to look up from the privacy of reading to test live human waters again. "For the past three months I've lived like a moth in a towel [reading]. Did I tell you I can make lovely, rich, savoury vegetable soup? Tonight we shall have macaroni au gratin and my lover's [family's] cream. . . . I would like to ask, quite simply, do you still love me? Remember how I waved that day in Meck Sqre. Do love me. Virginia." Love me. This letter to Ethel, nearly her last to her long-standing playmate, connects the private solace of books back to life. Woolf looks up from hidden comforts and talks of food and feeling: macaroni, soup, mutual memories. She's trembling as she takes her risk. "Do you still love me? . . . Do." That's the interplay between books and life that Virignia always knew to exist. We are social creatures who foster ideal intimacy in the written word; in life, we test, and try, and race after those attractive images.

Epilogue

I T'S EASY TO THINK Virginia Woolf lived a life that felt as big as it feels to us now. It's easy to inflate old heroes—as if they knew what they'd leave behind as they lived. But few of them did. Moments simply felt like moments. Virginia was often unhappy.

It's hard for me to *feel* how she could have been unhappy. It's hard to think of how someone created something that's been so meaningful for so many readers, but doubted her significance as she did it. Most of the time, Woolf didn't know what she was creating for other people. She had a vague idea—but couldn't know how her words would affect people like me, her unknown readers, years later.

· · · · ·

I'M RIDING IN THE subway after class, tired, and most of my students are riding home on different lines. I assigned a third of her book tonight.

So life goes on. I stand in the subway car, pulling close and pushing away from the pole, watching colors flash by outside the window, until my stop comes. I go to a café next to my apartment, where I often go to read. Today I'm outside, ordering wine and a tuna sandwich. It's spring.

When I think of the day I've been through, I remember arranging my papers at the desk, the window in the classroom—and a moment that makes me embarrassed of my teaching. I made a gesture too boldly today, standing in front of the room, seeking my students' interest. This gesture is what I always do when teaching Virginia's book *To the Lighthouse*. In order to explain the lighthouse beam, I flash my fists, open, closed, open, closed, around the room. A few years ago I held the room's attention doing it, so I've relied on that same gesture since—and I usually see myself performing as if from outside myself, hoping for that moment when they admire my clarity. Now I remember and hate my silly gesture: the flashing hands, the squared hips, the grin. I feel hypocritical. I ask my students to read novels independently, but need them to get me completely.

The rush I get teaching feels bitter now. I watch people on the sidewalk, pick at my sandwich, and think of Candice, a student who has a strong enough ego to roll her eyes (she once silently laughed) when I perform.

· · · · ·

I KNOW PARTS OF Candice's personality through her responses. She's creative enough to defend what she thinks. That autonomy can also sting, because she thinks of independence as too much like confrontation. I have the sense she'd like me more if we just slowed down.

She knows the part of me that teaches. I know snapshots of her—her classroom voice, her midterm paper, the stack of bracelets on her wrist. Hurt by and curious of her private life, I'm thinking of her now.

· · · · ·

THIS IS THE SORT of long-distance communication that fascinated Woolf. We speak in bits; we make contact; but—even in more intimate cases—we only understand pieces of each other. We are engaged in a struggle to impress and affect one another. Communication is complicated by the fact that we listen by apperceiving, which means we edit new insights for the images, scenes, or assumptions that already populate our minds. We hear what connects with what we already know. As Woolf writes in *Mrs. Dalloway*, though we exchange complex information when we talk, we also mute personal differences as we leave. We are "attached to [each other] by a thin thread . . . which . . . get[s] thinner and thinner as [we walk] across" town, recasting conversations to fit present needs. This fact sets limits on how much we see inside each other.

· · · · ·

LIKE WOOLF AND LIKE the characters in her stories, I often feel a deep desire to be *understood correctly*. Woolf shares her vision of the limitations of that dream in the middle section of *To the Lighthouse,* in which she spans ten years and—in an impersonal narrative voice—reports the most loved characters dead. The narrative sweeps coolly through their emptied summerhouse, scanning their abandoned books, their pots, their clothes. The lighthouse, as it always did, marks time across the bay, cycling light through the living room windows.

As we float through an empty house, we remember how the family, the Ramsays, interacted, affected, or touched each other. What resonates takes shape behind their backs. We see Mrs. Ramsay's shawl and coat, abandoned; she doesn't know how her friends, sorting through those scraps she left, re-create old scenes. Friends' memories are the energy that sustains her. The woman is not in control but has abandoned her legacy to those who knew her. Her conversations and gestures mattered in some way; they now build the woman who spans through time.

The sense of mourning in this section casts a shadow on our own lives. Like I remember Mrs. Ramsay, people will remember a "me" I don't fully know or control. Someone will look at my old bag and remember a laugh I don't remember making; they'll resurrect a moodier or wittier or shier person than I claim I am. That's what legacy is, Woolf says. It's being involved in, without fully understanding, the history we build with each other. Here Woolf suggests a moral surrender of control: We can love, without completely knowing, the story we're producing as we go.

In terms of making contact, Woolf focuses on the tough but important game of speech. You can see the drama again in my nervousness in the classroom, when I'm trying to tell students like the tough-minded Candice what feels so clear, or full, or personal inside when I read Woolf's books. Speaking my part feels risky because I don't like, know, or always agree with how others receive me.

You put together a description of your inside world and send it out; once that's done, you've got nothing to do but to trust in the autonomy of the other person.

A student thinks differently than I do—she loves parts of the novel that don't interest me as much. I don't control the ideas we finally shape together, or what parts of our conversation finally matter to her.

But Woolf also wrote all of her books—and her act of sharing strikes a parallel I want to live by. Your willingness to reveal what's inside—and to trust in others to think on their own—is the challenge of living deeply throughout Woolf's work. She puts it in her plots. In many of her stories, characters sit at the fringe of conversation; and speaking marks the climax. These characters quiver with a privately cradled challenge: *Should I talk even if it means miscommunication?* Think of what happens, again, in the classroom. If I speak, I at least take heart that I'm doing *something*. At least I'm not stingy with what I think; and if the conversation's honest, we let each other be original, and so do something to put a fresh idea into the world. We make meaning by trusting others to build with us.

· · · · ·

WOOLF HAD THAT COURAGE to write; she spent more time and effort sharing her inner vision than almost anyone in history. She granted her readers sovereignty in the right to read. That is, books like these—which aren't overly sarcastic, caught up in adventure plots, or safely cradled in convention—are a contract. She's expecting us to turn down the outside volume, to listen to her perspective. She tells us how she sees experience; and we extend her legacy by attempting the sort of empathy she practiced. The effort between two well-intentioned minds constructs and extends what humans can give to the world.

At the end of her life, Woolf suffered a terrible bout of doubt, feeling less heard than she ever had. That sinking, which led to her suicide, was the flip side to the faith she normally kept. There is probably no other greater model on Earth of a woman who managed to send out interior light for others to witness; in doing it, she left a vivid portrait of a human mind. This was an ethical exposure: a rallying call to ongoing observation, to humble acknowledgment of each other. She demands the guts to look deeply at the people around us. We comfort each other, she said, by hosting each other; by watching who struggles, intuiting what they mean, and sustaining the images that move us.

Notes

INTRODUCTION

xv **"Observe perpetually . . .":** Virginia Woolf, *The Diary of Virginia Woolf*, 5 vols., ed. Anne Olivier Bell (San Diego: Harcourt Brace Jovanovich, Inc., 1977–1984), 5: 357–8.

CHAPTER 1: SPEAK UP

9 **"Why not. . . . Let [him]":** Virginia Woolf, *To the Lighthouse* (San Diego: Harvest/Harcourt Brace Jovanovich, Inc., 1981), 95–96.
10 **"For the hundred and fiftieth . . .":** Ibid., 92.

CHAPTER 2: ACCEPT SOLITUDE

22 **She warns us . . . :** Virginia Woolf, *The Moment and Other Essays*, 2nd ed. (San Diego: Harcourt Brace & Company, 1975), 15; 14; 16.

22 **"In the rough and tumble . . ."**: Woolf, *Lighthouse*, 199.

25 **"a central oyster . . ."**: Virginia Woolf, *The Death of the Moth and Other Essays* (San Diego: Harcourt Brace & Company, 1942 [1970]), 22.

25 **"one's friends were attached . . ."**: Virginia Woolf, *Mrs. Dalloway* (San Diego: Harvest/Harcourt Brace & Company, 1981), 112.

26 **"violently two opposite . . ."**: Woolf, *Lighthouse*, 102.

28 **"sinking; he was . . ."**: Virginia Woolf, *The Years* (San Diego: Harvest/Harcourt Brace & Company, 1969), 375.

28 **"[So this] is what . . ."**: Woolf, *Lighthouse*, 173.

28 **" 'You' and 'I' . . ."**: Ibid., 179.

29 **"Sydney comes in . . ."**: Woolf, *The Diary* (1978), 2: 193.

31 **"drew a line . . ."**: Woolf, *Lighthouse*, 209.

32 **"fifty pairs of eyes . . ."**: Ibid., 198.

33 **"The pin [that needs] . . ."**: Woolf, *The Death of the Moth*, 8.

34 **"Continuity and Change in Personality"**: Walter Mischel, "Continuity and Change in Personality," *American Psychologist* 24, no. 11 (1969): 1012–1018.

34 **"The soul . . ."**: Virginia Woolf to Ethel Smyth, 1937, in *The Letters of Virginia Woolf*, 6 vols., eds. Nigel Nicolson and Joanne Trautmann (New York: Harcourt Brace Jovanovich, Inc., 1975–1980), 6: 112.

35 **What they found was:** R. Sherlock Campbell and James Pennebaker, "The secret life of pronouns: Flexibility in writing style and physical health," *Psychological Science* 14, no. 1 (2003): 60–65.

CHAPTER 3: SHUT DOWN

38 **"Suppose one's normal pulse . . .":** Woolf, *The Diary* (1978), 2: 224.

38 **"sensitive to the actual . . .":** Leonard Woolf, *Downhill All the Way: An Autobiography of the Years 1919–1939* (New York: Harcourt, Brace & World, 1967), 98–99.

41 **"You can't hate my . . .":** Virginia Woolf, *Moments of Being*, 2nd ed., ed. Jeanne Schulkind (San Diego: Harvest/Harcourt Brace & Company, 1985), 212.

43 **"Sit and soak . . .":** Woolf, *The Death of the Moth*, 8.

43 **Archibald MacLeish:** Archibald MacLeish, "Psychological Warfare," *Nation* 156, no. 10 (March 1943): 324.

47 **"killing some . . . insect . . .":** Virginia Woolf, *A Room of One's Own* (San Diego: Harcourt Brace & Company, 1981), 31.

48 **"Are you kidding? . . .":** "Dylan Meets the Press," *Village Voice*, March 3, 1965, http://www.interferenza.com/bcs/interw/65-mar3.htm (accessed December 16, 2006).

49 **"load and aim . . .":** Virginia Woolf, *The Second Common Reader*, ed. Andrew McNeillie (New York: Harcourt Brace Jovanovich, Inc., 1960), 270.

CHAPTER 4: TAKE ON CHALLENGING FRIENDSHIPS

52 **"I am the most . . .":** Smyth is rumored to have said this young in life, and repeated the idea in writing later. Queertheory.com, http://www.queertheory.com/histories/s/smyth_dame_ethel.htm (accessed October 8, 2006).

53 **"Well, what are you . . ."**: Woolf to Smyth, 1933, *The Letters of Virginia Woolf* (1979), 5: 187.

53 **"I don't think I . . ."** Quentin Bell, *Virignia Woolf: A Biography*, 2 vols. (New York: Harcourt Brace Jovanovich, Inc., 1972), 2: 151.

54 **"generous and free . . ."**: Louise Collis, *Impetuous Heart: The Story of Ethel Smyth* (London: William Kimber, 1984), 182.

54 **"To the casual onlooker . . ."**: Woolf to Smyth, 1931, *The Letters of Virginia Woolf*, 5: 329.

54 **"I think [you are] . . ."**: Woolf to Smyth, 1934, *The Letters of Virginia Woolf*, 5: 279.

54 **"periods of [love] . . ."**: Leo Tolstoy, *The Kreutzer Sonata,* http://etext.library.adelaide.edu.au/t/tolstoy/leo/t65kr/chapter17.html (accessed October 8, 2006).

56 **The psychologist W. Ray Crozier:** In studying cultural practices, literature, and psychology clients, Crozier equates our ability to sit with shame with an ability to better understand how we interact with others. See Ray Crozier, "Self-conscious in shame: The role of the 'other'," *Journal for the Theory of Social Behaviour* 28, no. 3 (September 1998): 271–286.

61 **"stark naked, brown . . ."**: Woolf to Vita, 1925, *The Letters of Virginia Woolf* (1977), 3: 198.

61 **"[you] longeared owl . . ."**: Woolf to Vita, 1926, *The Letters of Virginia Woolf*, 3: 231.

62 **Gary Fine and Lori Holyfield:** Gary Fine and Lori Holyfield, "Secrecy, trust, and dangerous leisure: Generating group cohesion in voluntary organizations," *Social Psychology Quarterly* 59, no. 1 (March 1996): 22–38.

62 **Rutger Engels, Catrin Finkenauer:** Tom Frijins, Catrin Finkenauer, Ad Vermulst, and Rutger Engels, "Keeping Secrets from Parents: Longitudinal Associations of Secrecy in Adolescence," *Journal of Youth and Adolescence* 34, no. 2 (April 2005): 137–148.

63 **"I wanted to exclaim . . .":** Vita Sackville-West to Virginia Woolf, 1938, in *The Letters of Vita Sackville-West to Virginia Woolf*, eds. Louise DeSalvo and Mitchell A. Leaska (New York: William Morrow and Company, Inc., 1985), 413.

63 **"As for myself . . .":** Woolf to Vita, 1940, *The Letters of Virginia Woolf* (1980), 6: 385.

CHAPTER 5: FIND STEADY SUPPORT

67 **"broaden-and-build theory":** Barbara Fredrickson, "What Good are Positive Emotions?," *Review of General Psychology. Special Issue: New Directions in Research on Emotion* 2, no. 3 (September 1998): 300–319.

68 **"L. has trained . . .":** Woolf, *The Diary* (1984), 5: 248.

69 **"I have known people . . .":** Leonard Woolf, *Downhill*, 149.

71 **He's a buoy:** Woolf, *The Diary* (1984), 5: 127; 133; 151; 159; 20; 159.

74 **"the best mode . . .":** Franz Kafka, *The Basic Kafka with Introduction by Erich Heller*, 2nd ed. (New York: Washington Square Press, 1979), xii.

CHAPTER 6: WORK HARD, EVEN WITHOUT A SIGN OF SUCCESS

75 **"sterile . . . refined . . .":** Published under psudonym Simon Pure. *Virginia Woolf: The Critical Heritage*, ed. Robin Majumdar and Allen McLaurin (London and Boston: Routledge & Kegan Paul, 1975), 132.

75 **"bloodless" novels "approaching mush":** Ibid., 267–268.

76 **"continues until the end . . .":** Ibid., 165.

77 **"Happiness—what I . . .":** Woolf, *The Diary* (1977), 1: 269.

78 **"the Press . . . prevents brooding . . .":** Ibid., 2: 308.

79 **"Things don't happen . . .":** Ibid., 3: 127.

80 **"I'm not going to . . .":** Ibid., 2: 168.

80 **"Novels do come . . .":** Woolf, *A Room*, 73.

82 **"cheeks burn":** Woolf, *The Diary*, 2: 17.

82 **"If we didn't live . . .":** Ibid., 2: 308–309.

83 **"Writing in English . . .":** In a letter of September 5, 1918. "James Joyce" in Wikiquote, http://en.wikiquote.org/wiki/James_Joyce (accessed October 8, 2006).

83 **In his "equal-odds" rule:** Dean Simonton, "Creative Productivity: A Predictive and Explanatory Model of Career Trajectories and Landmarks," *Psychological Review* 104, no. 1 (January 1997): 66–89.

85 **"The day after my . . .":** Woolf, *The Diary*, 2: 13–14.

85 **"I should say a . . .":** Ibid., 2: 263.

85 **"discover[ed] what I call . . .":** Ibid., 2: 272.

CHAPTER 7: LIE TO ENCOURAGE YOUR FRIENDS

91 **"If by our means . . .":** Woolf, *The Second Common Reader*, 270.

93 **"Now I was no longer . . .":** Woolf, *The Diary*, 5: 29.

94 **"Extraordinarily good . . ."** Ibid., 5: 30.

95 **Virginia's book earnings:** Leonard Woolf, *Downhill*, 144.

97 **"What laws can be laid down . . ."** Woolf, *The Second Common Reader*, 258.

97 **"It may be one . . .":** Ibid., 263.

98 **a "shooting gallery . . .":** Ibid., 270.

99 **The Mystery of Picasso:** Clouzot, Henri-Georges, *Le Mystère Picasso*. Produced and directed by Henri-Georges Clouzot (France: Filmsonor S.A., 1956).

99 **"I brood more over . . ."** Charles Matthews, "Gustave Flaubert's World: Biography of Madame Bovary's Creator Gives Vivid Sense of the Man and his 19th-century Milieu," book review posted on March 31, 2004, http://www.chron.com/disp/story.mpl/life/books/reviews/3760307.html (accessed October 8, 2006).

CHAPTER 8: FIND A POLITICAL VOICE

102 **"an attitude of . . .":** Virginia Woolf, *Three Guineas* (New York: Harcourt, Brace and Company, 1938), 163.

104 **"hawking his conscience":** Woolf, *The Diary,* 4: 345.

104 **"tub thumper":** Woolf, *The Diary,* 3: 80–81.

104 **"It's odd to feel . . .":** Woolf to Smyth, 1940, *The Letters of Virginia Woolf*, 6: 430.

104 **A psychologist helps:** Martin Seligman developed his idea with the help of Bruce Overmier, Byron Campbell, and others. See Martin Seligman, Steven Maier, and James Greer, "Alleviation of Learned Helplessness in the Dog," *Journal of Abnormal Psychology* 73, no. 3 (1968): 256–262.

106 **"It seems plain . . .":** Woolf, *Three Guineas*, 13.

106 **"a gulf so deeply . . .":** Woolf, *Three Guineas*, 5.

107 **"suppressed [female] poet . . .":** Woolf, *A Room of One's Own*, 49.

CHAPTER 9: BE AWARE OF PREJUDICE

114 **"a board is not . . ."**: Woolf, *Three Guineas*, 76.

115 **"a very mighty power . . ."**: Ibid., 79.

116 **Stereotype Threat:** Claude Steele and Joshua Aronson, "Stereotype threat and the intellectual test performance of African Americans," *Journal of Personality and Social Psychology* 69, no. 5 (November 1995): 797–811.

117 **Michael Inzlicht and Talia Ben-Zeev:** Michael Inzlicht and Talia Ben-Zeev, "Do High-Achieving Female Students Underperform in Private? The Implications of Threatening Environments on Intellectual Processing," *Journal of Educational Psychology* 95, no. 4 (December 2003): 796–805.

119 **"ah jes kept . . ."**: Lauren Sklaroff, "Joe Louis and the Construction of a Black American Hero," The Poetics of Definition: Racial Representation in 20th Century America, http://epsilon3.georgetown.edu/~coventrm/asa2000/panel1/sklaroff.html#foot6 (accessed October 8, 2006).

CHAPTER 10: CHANGE ROUTINES

124 **"This or that . . ."**: Woolf, *A Room*, 40.

125 **"Yesterday I spent . . ."**: Woolf, *The Diary*, 3: 212.

128 **"I must note . . ."**: Ibid., 2: 108.

128 **"I must hurriedly . . ."**: Ibid., 5: 108.

130 **"Suppose, I bought . . ."**: Ibid., 5: 358.

130 **"Oh vanity, vanity! . . ."**: Ibid, 2: 63.

130 **people listen to happy music:** G. Sutherland, B. Newman, and S. Rachman, "Experimental investigations of the relations between mood and intrusive unwanted cognitions," *British Journal of Medical Psychology*, 55, no. 2 (June 1982): 127–138.

131 **"I predict that . . .":** Woolf, *The Diary*, 5: 308.

133 **"their relationship to each . . ."** Ibid., 1: 140.

135 **"Dinner last night . . .":** Ibid., 5: 230.

138 **"cheeks of paté . . .":** Woolf to Vita, 1926, *The Letters of Virginia Woolf*, 3: 236.

140 **"The most important thing . . .":** Woolf, *The Diary*, 4: 101.

CHAPTER 11: READ YOUR PARTNER

145 **"the land dwindling . . ."** Woolf, *Lighthouse*, 69.

CHAPTER 12: MAKE USE OF TIME

153 **"the excitement of life . . .":** The quotation comes from Vita's diary entry on February 22, 1923, cited in Vanessa Curtis, *Virginia Woolf's Women* (London: Robert Hale, 2003), 155.

154 **"one sees through . . ."** : Woolf, *Moments of Being*, 98.

155 **"moments of being . . .":** Ibid., 70.

156 **The psychologist McWelling Todman:** McWelling Todman, "Boredom and Psychotic Disorders: Cognitive and Motivational Issues," *Psychiatry: Interpersonal and Biological Processes* 66, no. 2 (Summer 2003): 146–167.

158 **"but directly the word . . .":** Virginia Woolf, *A Haunted House and Other Short Stories* (San Diego: Harcourt Brace Jovanovich, Inc., 1972), 142.

159 **"I receive these sudden . . ."** Woolf, *Moments of Being*, 72.

161 **"This attempt at . . .":** Woolf, *The Diary*, 1: 55.

CHAPTER 13: READ AND BE MORE

164 "not to throw . . .": Woolf, *The Second Common Reader*, 263.

165 "seeking meaning . . ." Woolf, *The Diary*, 1: 192.

168 "Little negligible words . . .": Woolf, *The Years*, 50.

171 "like the alphabet . . .": Woolf, *Lighthouse*, 34.

172 "fortified him . . .": Ibid., 120.

176 "They had nothing . . .": Ibid., 119.

176 "Don't interrupt me . . .": Ibid., 119, then 121.

178 "How odd it is . . .": Woolf to Vita, 1926, *The Letters of Virginia Woolf*, 3: 253.

179 "We owe a great . . ." Virginia Woolf, *Collected Essays*, 4 vols (New York: Harcourt Brace & World, Inc., 1967), 2: 37.

181 "It's a good thing . . .": Woolf to Smyth, 1940, *The Letters of Virginia Woolf*, 6: 399.

182 "I've written you": Ibid., 6: 467.

EPILOGUE

188 "attached to . . .": Woolf, *Mrs. Dalloway*, 112.